MUSIC THEORY BE~~~~~

ULTIMATE MUSIC THEORY

G♪G

By Glory St. Germain ARCT RMT MYCC UMTC &
Shelagh McKibbon-U'Ren RMT UMTC

Introducing the Ultimate Music Theory Family!

So-La

Ti-Do

Meet So-La! So-La loves to sing and dance.

She is expressive, creative and loves to tell stories through music!

So-La feels music in her heart. She loves to teach, compose and perform.

Meet Ti-Do! Ti-Do loves to count and march.

He is rhythmic, consistent and loves the rules of music theory!

Ti-Do feels music in his hands and feet. He loves to analyze, share tips and conduct.

So-La & Ti-Do will guide you through Mastering Music Theory!

Enriching Lives Through Music Education

ISBN: 978-1-927641-22-4

Ultimate Music Theory - *The Way to Score Success!*

The Ultimate Music Theory Beginner Series consists of 3 workbooks: A, B and C.
These workbooks provide young students with a solid foundation in theory and piano pedagogy.

Teachers and Students are encouraged to play each theory lesson on the piano to develop and strengthen the connection between theory (what is seen) and piano (what is heard and played). These techniques will develop strong musicianship skills in Ear Training and Sight Reading.

At the end of each of the 12 lessons is an accumulative Review Test that reinforces all concepts learned from the very first Lesson. To support a stress-free learning environment, the Review Tests are not graded. Simply CHECK ✓ each **Review with So-La & Ti-Do** upon successful completion.

Published in 2018 by Gloryland Publishing
Printed in Canada.
GlorylandPublishing.com

Library and Archives Canada Cataloguing in Publication
Ultimate Music Theory Beginner A B C Series / Glory St. Germain and Shelagh McKibbon-U'Ren

Gloryland Publishing - Ultimate Music Theory Series:

GP - TBA	ISBN: 978-1-927641-21-7	Ultimate Music Theory Beginner Level A
GP - TBB	ISBN: 978-1-927641-22-4	Ultimate Music Theory Beginner Level B
GP - TBC	ISBN: 978-1-927641-23-1	Ultimate Music Theory Beginner Level C
GP - UP1	ISBN: 978-0-9809556-6-8	Ultimate Prep 1 Rudiments
GP - UP1A	ISBN: 978-0-9809556-9-9	Ultimate Prep 1 Rudiments Answer Book
GP - UP2	ISBN: 978-0-9809556-7-5	Ultimate Prep 2 Rudiments
GP - UP2A	ISBN: 978-0-9813101-0-7	Ultimate Prep 2 Rudiments Answer Book
GP- UBR	ISBN: 978-0-9813101-3-8	Ultimate Basic Rudiments
GP - UBRA	ISBN: 978-0-9813101-4-5	Ultimate Basic Answer Book
GP - UIR	ISBN: 978-0-9813101-5-2	Ultimate Intermediate Rudiments
GP - UIRA	ISBN: 978-0-9813101-6-9	Ultimate Intermediate Answer Book
GP - UAR	ISBN: 978-0-9813101-7-6	Ultimate Advanced Rudiments
GP - UARA	ISBN: 978-0-9813101-8-3	Ultimate Advanced Answer Book
GP - UCR	ISBN: 978-0-9813101-1-4	Ultimate Complete Rudiments
GP - UCRA	ISBN: 978-0-9813101-2-1	Ultimate Complete Answer Book

♫ **Note: The Ultimate Music Theory Program includes the UMT Workbook Series, Exam Series and Supplemental Series to help students successfully prepare for national theory exams.**

UltimateMusicTheory.com

So-La

ULTIMATE MUSIC THEORY

Music Theory Beginner B

Ti-Do

Table of Contents

Ultimate Music Theory Guide & Chart - Beginner B

Ultimate Music Theory - *The Way to Score Success!*

Lesson 1　　　Black and White Keys on the Keyboard

BLACK KEYS - LANDMARK GROUPS OF TWO and THREE
WHITE KEY PATTERNS - C, D, E and F, G, A, B

Each key has a different pitch. The pitch is how LOW or HIGH a note sounds.

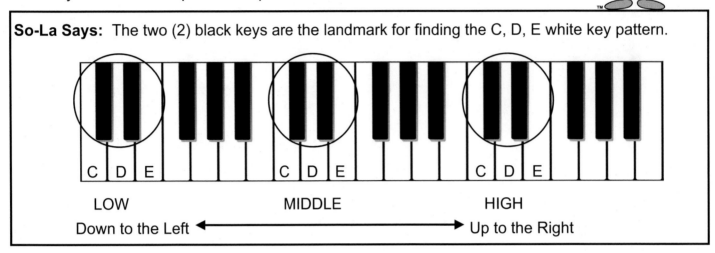

So-La Says: The two (2) black keys are the landmark for finding the C, D, E white key pattern.

| C | D | E | | C | D | E | | C | D | E |

LOW　　　　　　　　MIDDLE　　　　　　　HIGH

Down to the Left ←————————————→ Up to the Right

♫ **Ti-Do Tip:** When moving from left to right UP the keyboard, the pitch gets HIGHER in sound.

1. Circle the groups of 2 black keys. Name the white keys C, D, E going up - LOW, MIDDLE, HIGH.

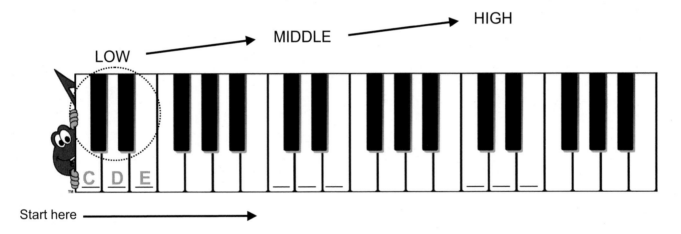

♫ **Ti-Do Tip:** When moving from right to left DOWN the keyboard, the pitch gets LOWER in sound.

2. Circle the groups of 2 black keys. Name the white keys E, D, C going down - HIGH, MIDDLE, LOW.

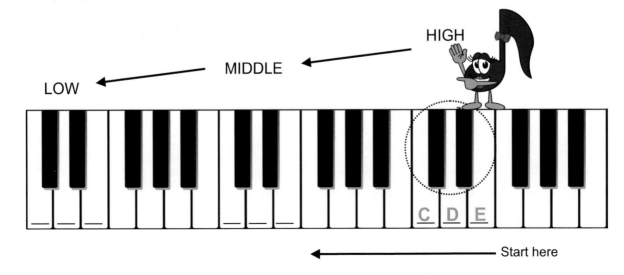

BLACK and WHITE KEYS - PITCH - LOW SOUND, MIDDLE SOUND and HIGH SOUND

So-La Says: The three (3) black keys are the landmark for finding the F, G, A, B white key pattern.

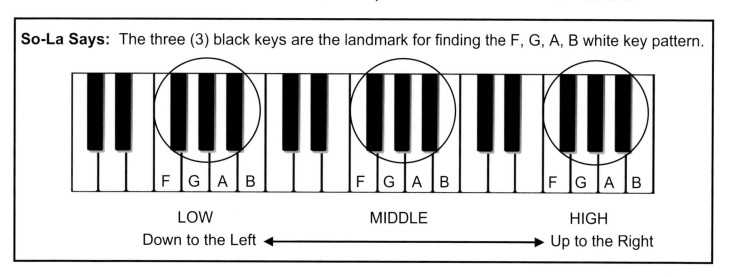

LOW   MIDDLE   HIGH

Down to the Left ←——————————————→ Up to the Right

♫ **Ti-Do Tip:** When moving from left to right UP the keyboard, the pitch gets HIGHER in sound.

1. Circle the groups of 3 black keys. Name the white keys F, G, A, B going up - LOW, MIDDLE, HIGH.

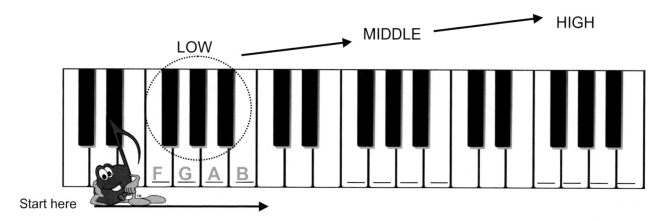

♫ **Ti-Do Tip:** When moving from right to left DOWN the keyboard, the pitch gets LOWER in sound.

2. Circle the groups of 3 black keys. Name the white keys B, A, G, F going down - HIGH, MIDDLE, LOW.

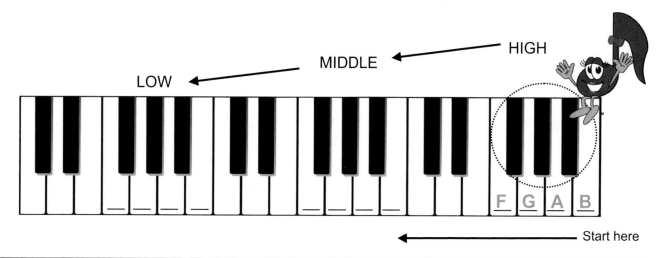

♫ **Ti-Do Time:** Play (on the piano) the groups of 2 or 3 black keys. Explore playing from low to middle to high and from high to middle to low.

Play (on the piano) the white key patterns C, D, E and F, G, A, B. Explore playing from low to middle to high and from high to middle to low. Say the names of the white keys as you play.

The **MUSICAL ALPHABET** consists of 7 letter names **A, B, C, D, E, F, G**.

Going UP, the Musical Alphabet repeats **A, B, C, D, E, F, G** and again **A, B, C, D, E, F, G**.

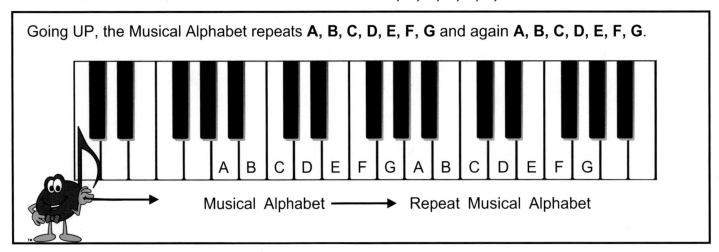

♫ **Ti-Do Tip:** The WHITE keys repeat the 7 letter names of the Musical Alphabet over and over. When moving from left to right UP the keyboard, the sound gets HIGHER in pitch.

1. Write the Musical Alphabet A, B, C, D, E, F, G going UP the keyboard from LOW to HIGH.

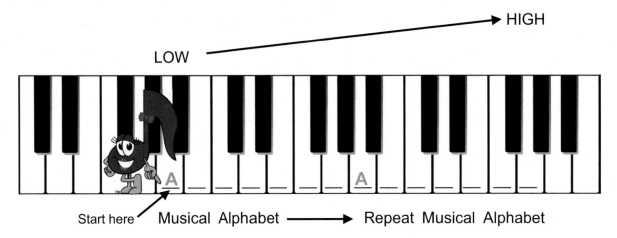

2. Name all the white keys marked with a ☺ going UP the keyboard from left to right.

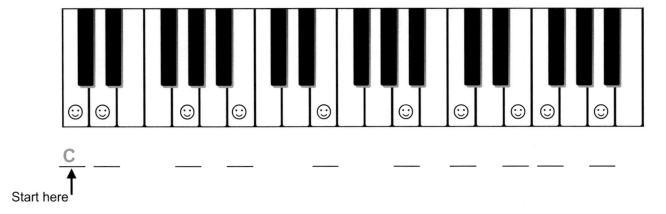

3. Write the Musical Alphabet (A, B, C, D, E, F, G) twice (2 times) going UP. Play (on the piano) the white keys A, B, C, D, E, F, G going UP the keyboard. Say the names as you play.

A ___ ___ ___ ___ ___ ___   A ___ ___ ___ ___ ___ ___

Start here   Musical Alphabet ——→ Repeat Musical Alphabet

WHITE KEYS GOING DOWN G, F, E, D, C, B, A

Going DOWN, the Musical Alphabet repeats **G, F, E, D, C, B, A** and again **G, F, E, D, C, B, A**.

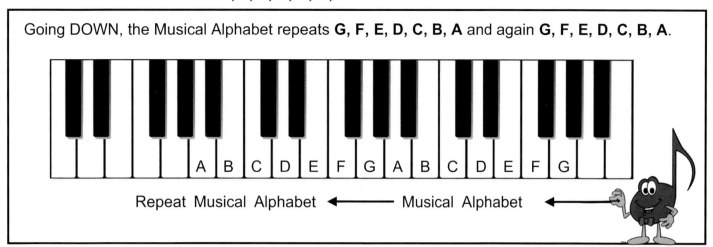

♫ **Ti-Do Tip:** The WHITE keys repeat the 7 letter names of the Musical Alphabet over and over. When moving from right to left DOWN the keyboard, the sound gets LOWER in pitch.

1. Write the Musical Alphabet G, F, E, D, C, B, A going DOWN the keyboard from HIGH to LOW.

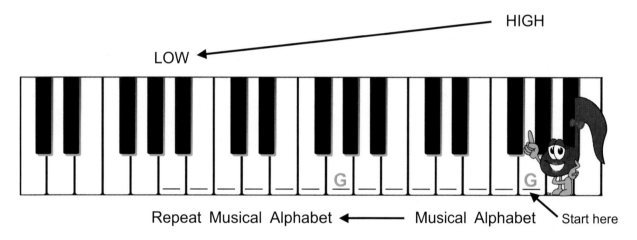

2. Name all the white keys marked with a ☺ going DOWN the keyboard from right to left.

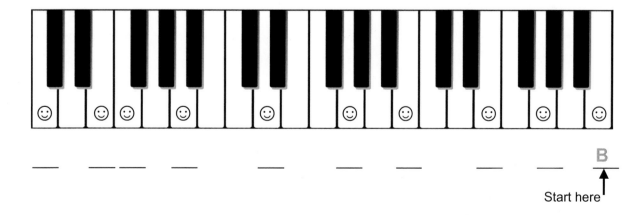

3. Write the Musical Alphabet (G, F, E, D, C, B, A) twice (2 times) going DOWN. Play (on the piano) the white keys G, F, E, D, C, B, A going DOWN the keyboard. Say the names as you play.

Lesson 1 Review with So-La & Ti-Do

Check:

1. Starting down LOW and going UP the Musical Alphabet, add the missing letter names.

A ___ C D ___ F G ___ B ___ D E ___ ___ A B ___ ___ E ___ ___

Start here ↑ →

SAY the Musical Alphabet going UP 3 times from A.

Have Fun! Start with a LOW voice and go UP higher in pitch to end with a HIGH voice.

2. Starting down LOW and going UP the keyboard, add the missing letter names.

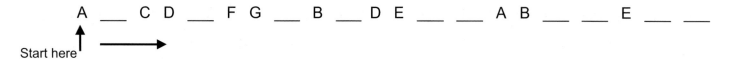

Start here ↑ →

PLAY the Musical Alphabet going UP 3 times from A. Say the letter names as you play.

Have Fun! Start with a LOW voice and go UP higher in pitch to end with a HIGH voice.

3. Starting up HIGH and going DOWN the Musical Alphabet, add the missing letter names.

A ___ C ___ E ___ G ___ B ___ D E ___ ___ A B ___ D ___ F G

← ↑ **Start here**

SAY the Musical Alphabet going DOWN 3 times from G.

Have Fun! Start with a HIGH voice and go DOWN lower in pitch to end with a LOW voice.

4. Starting up HIGH and going DOWN the keyboard, add the missing letter names.

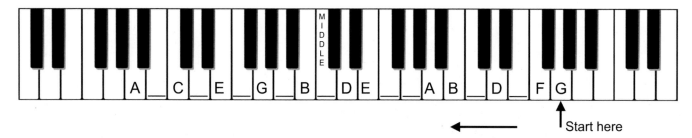

← ↑ **Start here**

PLAY the Musical Alphabet going DOWN 3 times from G. Say the letter names as you play.

Have Fun! Start with a HIGH voice and go DOWN lower in pitch to end with a LOW voice.

Lesson 1 Review Ultimate Sight Reading & Ear Training Games

1. WRITE the correct alphabet letter name to find each white key.
    WRITE the letter name directly on the keyboard. (Same letter name twice on each keyboard.)
    PLAY the white keys with the same alphabet letter name going UP or going DOWN on the piano.

_____ is the white key between the
2nd (middle) and 3rd (right) of the 3 black keys.

_____ is the white key on the
top right of the 3 black keys.

_____ is the white key on the
bottom left of the 2 black keys.

_____ is the white key in the
middle of the 2 black keys.

_____ is the white key on the
top right of the 2 black keys.

_____ is the white key on the
bottom left of the 3 black keys.

_____ is the white key between the
1st (bottom) and 2nd (middle) of the 3 black keys.

Imagine, Compose, Explore!

Imagine So-La and Ti-Do are giving Boat Rides!

Compose a song using the 2 and 3 black key groups.

Explore the sound as the waves go up HIGH & down LOW.

Boat Rides

Lesson 2   Treble Clef - Landmark Notes and Patterns

The **TREBLE CLEF** or **G CLEF** is drawn on the STAFF. Music notes written in the Treble Clef (or Treble Staff) are drawn as a circle (oval shape) called a Whole Note.

So-La Says: Treble Clef or G Clef on the Staff (5 lines & 4 spaces) has line notes & space notes.

Line 1 is the first line at the bottom (low) going up to Line 5 at the top (high).

Space 1 is the first space at the bottom (low) going up to Space 4 at the top (high).

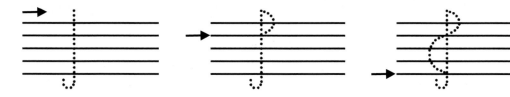

Line: 1   2   3   4   5   Space: 1   2   3   4

1. Draw (trace) the Treble Clef on the staff by using the following 4 steps.

Draw a "**J**" from above to below the staff.

Start at the top of the "**J**" and draw a "**P**" to line 4.

Draw a "**d**" from line 4 all the way down to line 1.

Circle up to line 3 and curl, finishing on line 2.

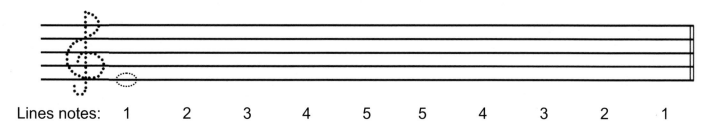

♫ **Ti-Do Tip:** Notes may be written as line notes or space notes. In the Treble Clef, when notes move UP the staff, the pitch gets HIGHER. When notes move DOWN the staff, the pitch gets LOWER.

2. Draw a Treble Clef at the beginning of the staff. Draw a whole note on each given line number.

Lines notes: 1   2   3   4   5   5   4   3   2   1

3. Draw a Treble Clef at the beginning of the staff. Draw a whole note in each given space number.

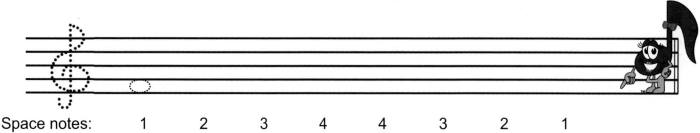

Space notes: 1   2   3   4   4   3   2   1

TREBLE CLEF or G CLEF - LANDMARK NOTES MIDDLE C and TREBLE G

Music notes written in the Treble Clef or G Clef are usually played with the Right Hand (RH).

Landmark Note Middle C - In the Treble Clef, Middle C is written below the Treble Staff on its own line. This line is called a LEDGER line. Ledger lines and staff lines are equal distances apart.

Landmark Note Treble G - In the Treble Clef (also called the G Clef), line 2 on the staff is the "**G**" line. The lines used to draw the Treble Clef cross line 2, the "**G**" line, four times.

As seen in music: As drawn by hand:

← Treble G line 2 →
← Middle C ledger line →

C   G   C   G

1. Fill in the blanks.

   a) The Treble Clef is also called the _____ Clef.

   b) Notes in the Treble Clef are usually played with the _____ Hand.

   c) The Landmark Notes in the Treble Clef are: Middle _____ and Treble _____.

♫ **Ti-Do Tip:** Always use a ruler to draw a straight ledger line below the Treble Staff for Middle C.

2. On each staff, draw a Treble Clef. Write the landmark notes Middle C and Treble G. Use whole notes. Draw a line connecting the notes Middle C and Treble G to the keyboard. Name the notes.

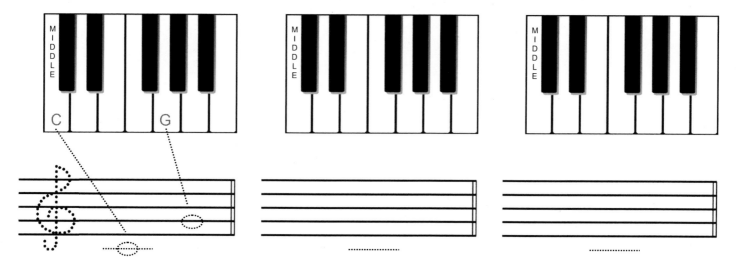

C   G   _____ _____   _____ _____

TREBLE CLEF - PITCH - MIDDLE SOUND and HIGH SOUND

Music written in the Treble Clef has a MIDDLE sound (pitch) UP to a HIGH sound (pitch).

Notes moving UP the staff are played moving up to the right on the keyboard, HIGHER in sound.
Notes moving DOWN the staff are played moving down to the left on the keyboard, LOWER in sound.

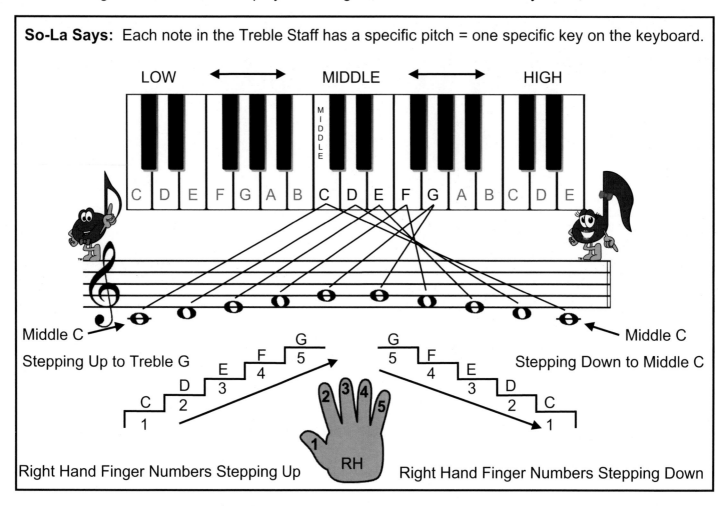

1. Each note on the staff has a specific _____ = one specific _____ on the keyboard.

2. Draw a line connecting the Treble Clef notes to the keyboard (at the correct pitch). Name the notes.

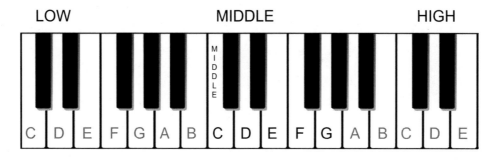

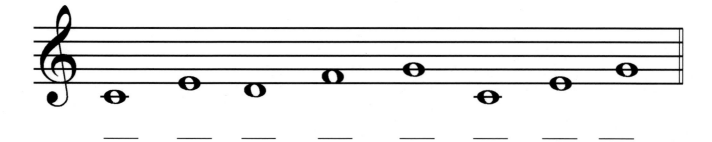

TREBLE CLEF PATTERNS - SAME, STEP and SKIP

So-La Says: Notes on the staff may be repeated as a SAME LINE or SAME SPACE note.
Notes may move by a STEP (UP or DOWN) or a SKIP (UP or DOWN).

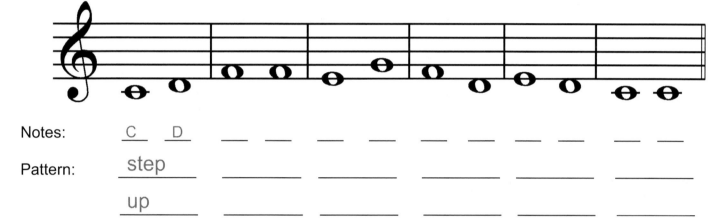

Notes:	G	G	E	F	D	F	F	F	G	F	E	C
Pattern:	Same Line		Step Up		Skip Up		Same Space		Step Down		Skip Down	

1. Name the notes. Name the pattern as: same (line or space), step (up or down), skip (up or down).

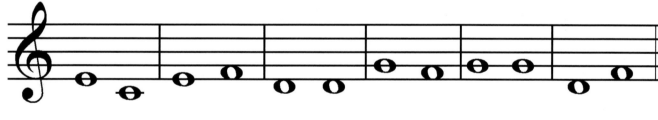

Notes: C D __ __ __ __ __ __ __ __ __ __

Pattern: step __ __ __ __ __ __ __ __ __ __

up __ __ __ __ __ __ __ __ __ __

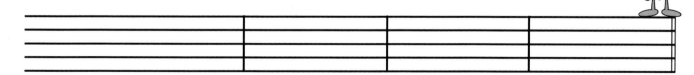

Notes: E C __ __ __ __ __ __ __ __ __ __

Pattern: skip __ __ __ __ __ __ __ __ __ __

down __ __ __ __ __ __ __ __ __ __

2. Draw a Treble Clef on the staff. Write the following patterns of notes. Use whole notes.
   Use a ruler to draw a ledger line below the Treble Staff when writing the line note Middle C.

Middle C (skip up) E   G (step down) F   D (same space) D   E (step up) F

Lesson 2 Review with So-La & Ti-Do

Check:

1. Circle the correct answer for each of the following:

   a) A staff has:

   　4 lines and 5 spaces　　　　or　　　　5 lines and 4 spaces

   b) How high or low a note sounds is the:

   　pitch　　　　or　　　　whole note

   c) The Treble Clef is also called the:

   　G Clef　　　　or　　　　F Clef

   d) In the Treble Clef, Middle C is written on:

   　a ledger line below the staff　　　or　　　a ledger line above the staff

   e) In the Treble Clef, Landmark Treble G is written on:

   　line 1　　　　or　　　　line 2

   f) The notes in the Treble Clef are usually played with the:

   　Left Hand　　　　or　　　　Right Hand

2. Draw a line connecting the Treble Clef notes to the keyboard (at the correct pitch).
   Name the notes. With your RH, play the notes and say the names of the notes out loud.

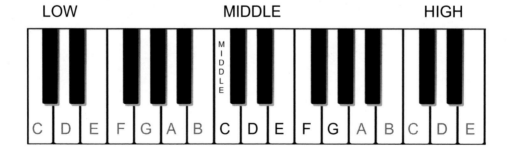

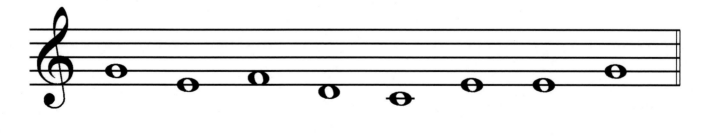

Lesson 2 Review Ultimate Sight Reading & Ear Training Games

1.   a) PICK 3 different colors of crayons. WRITE the name of one color for each pattern below.

Color: _____   _____   _____

same line or same space   step up or step down   skip up or skip down

   b) COLOR each ball pattern (same, step or skip) with the color that you picked for each pattern.

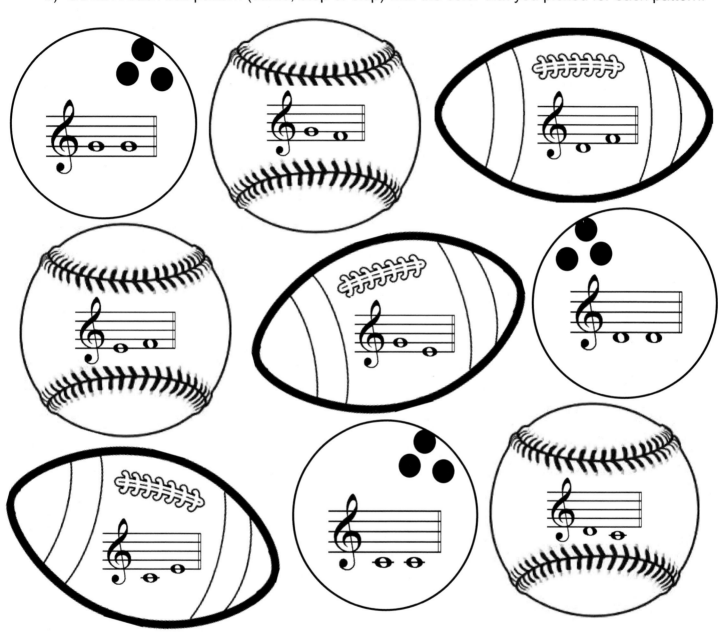

2.   PLAY BALL! Your Teacher will play the Treble Clef Patterns. Listen and name each pattern.

Imagine, **C**ompose, **E**xplore!

Imagine So-La and Ti-Do are playing sports!

Compose a song using the Treble Clef white keys C, D, E, F, G. Play them with your Right Hand.

Explore the sound. Is the ball bouncing in the same spot? Is the ball being rolled up and down? Is it being tossed back and forth?

Lesson 3   Bass Clef - Landmark Notes and Patterns

The **BASS CLEF** or **F CLEF** is drawn on the STAFF. Music notes written in the Bass Clef (or Bass Staff) are drawn as a circle (oval shape) called a Whole Note.

So-La Says: Bass Clef or F Clef on the Staff (5 lines & 4 spaces) has line notes & space notes.

Line 1 is the first line at the bottom (low) going up to Line 5 at the top (high).

Space 1 is the first space at the bottom (low) going up to Space 4 at the top (high).

Line: 1   2   3   4   5   Space: 1   2   3   4

1. Draw (trace) the Bass Clef on the staff by using the following 4 steps.

Draw a DOT on line 4.   Draw **half of a heart** up   Draw a DOT in space 4   Draw a DOT in space 3
This is the "**F**" line.   to line 5, down to space 1.   (above the "**F**" line).   (below the "**F**" line).

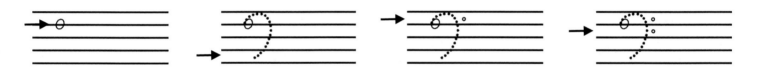

♫ **Ti-Do Tip:** Notes may be written as line notes or space notes. In the Bass Clef, when notes move UP the staff, the pitch gets HIGHER. When notes move DOWN the staff, the pitch gets LOWER.

2. Draw a Bass Clef at the beginning of the staff. Draw a whole note on each given line number.

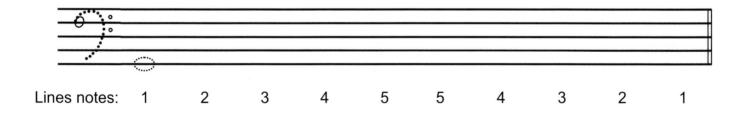

Lines notes: 1   2   3   4   5   5   4   3   2   1

3. Draw a Bass Clef at the beginning of the staff. Draw a whole note in each given space number.

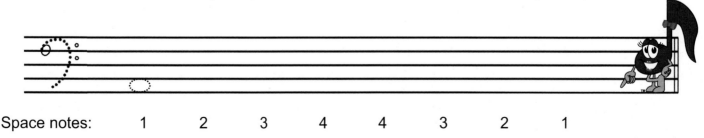

Space notes: 1   2   3   4   4   3   2   1

BASS CLEF or F CLEF - LANDMARK NOTES MIDDLE C and BASS F

Music notes written in the Bass Clef or F Clef are usually played with the Left Hand (LH).

Landmark Note Bass F - In the Bass Clef (also called the F Clef), line 4 on the staff is the "**F**" line. The two dots used to draw the Bass Clef are 1 above and 1 below line 4, the "F" line.

Landmark Note Middle C - In the Bass Clef, Middle C is written above the Bass Staff on its own line. This line is called a LEDGER line. Ledger lines and staff lines are equal distances apart.

As seen in music:

← Middle C ledger line →

← Bass F line 4 →

As drawn by hand:

F C

F C

1. Fill in the blanks.

   a) The Bass Clef is also called the _____ Clef.

   b) Notes in the Bass Clef are usually played with the _____ Hand.

   c) The Landmark Notes in the Bass Clef are: Bass _____ and Middle _____.

♫ **Ti-Do Tip:** Always use a ruler to draw a straight ledger line above the Bass Staff for Middle C.

2. On each staff, draw a Bass Clef. Write the landmark notes Bass F and Middle C. Use whole notes. Draw a line connecting the notes Bass F and Middle C to the keyboard. Name the notes.

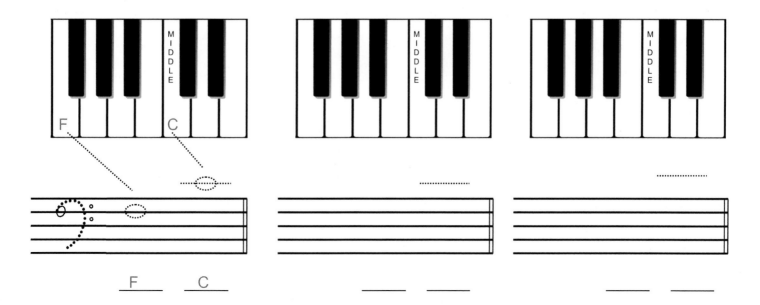

F C   _____ _____   _____ _____

BASS CLEF - PITCH - MIDDLE SOUND and LOW SOUND

Music written in the Bass Clef has a MIDDLE sound (pitch) DOWN to a LOW sound (pitch).

Notes moving UP the staff are played moving up to the right on the keyboard, HIGHER in sound.
Notes moving DOWN the staff are played moving down to the left on the keyboard, LOWER in sound.

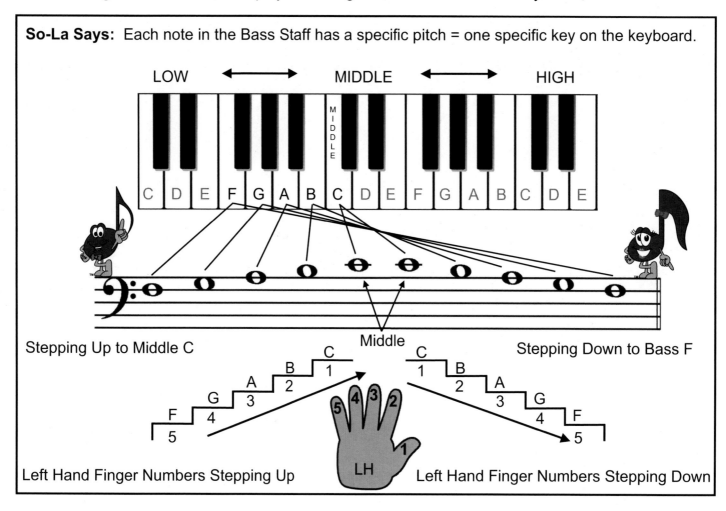

So-La Says: Each note in the Bass Staff has a specific pitch = one specific key on the keyboard.

LOW ← → MIDDLE ← → HIGH

Stepping Up to Middle C   Middle   Stepping Down to Bass F

Left Hand Finger Numbers Stepping Up   Left Hand Finger Numbers Stepping Down

1. Each note on the staff has a specific _____ = one specific _____ on the keyboard.

2. Draw a line connecting the Bass Clef notes to the keyboard (at the correct pitch). Name the notes.

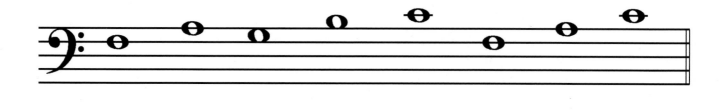

BASS CLEF PATTERNS - SAME, STEP and SKIP

So-La Says: Notes on the staff may be repeated as a SAME LINE or SAME SPACE note.
Notes may move by a STEP (UP or DOWN) or a SKIP (UP or DOWN).

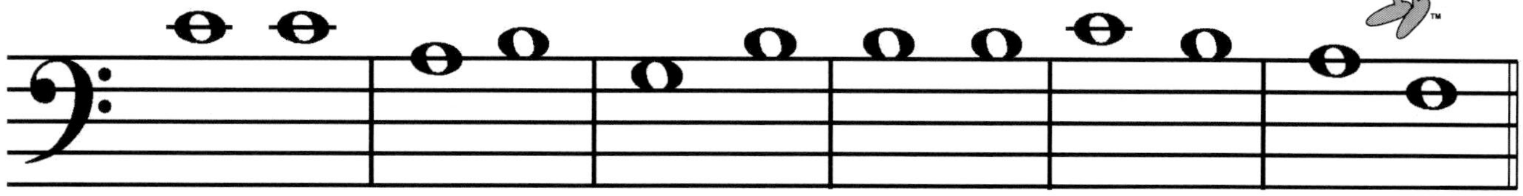

Notes:	C	C	A	B	G	B	B	B	C	B	A	F
Pattern:	Same Line		Step Up		Skip Up		Same Space		Step Down		Skip Down	

1. Name the notes. Name the pattern as: same (line or space), step (up or down), skip (up or down).

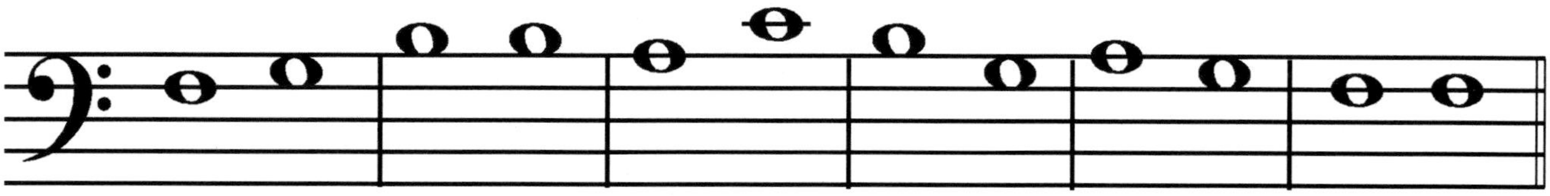

Notes: F   G   ___ ___   ___ ___   ___ ___   ___ ___   ___ ___

Pattern: step
up

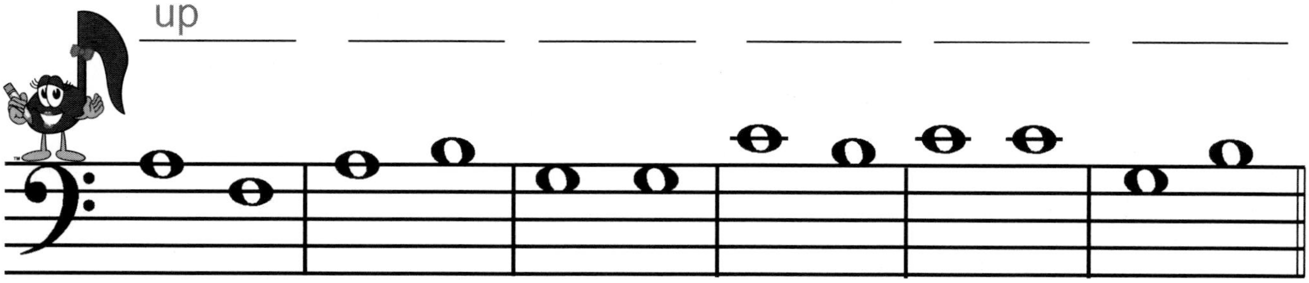

Notes: A   F   ___ ___   ___ ___   ___ ___   ___ ___   ___ ___

Pattern: skip
down

2. Draw a Bass Clef on the staff. Write the following patterns of notes. Use whole notes.
   Use a ruler to draw a ledger line above the Bass Staff when writing the line note Middle C.

Middle C (skip down) A   G (step up) A   F (same line) F   G (skip up) B

Lesson 3 Review with So-La & Ti-Do

Check:

1. Circle the correct answer for each of the following:

   a) A Music Note drawn as a circle (an oval) is called a:

   whole note   or   staff

   b) The lowest (bottom) line of the staff is numbered as:

   line 1   or   line 5

   c) The Bass Clef is also called the:

   G Clef   or   F Clef

   d) In the Bass Clef, Middle C is written on:

   a ledger line below the staff   or   a ledger line above the staff

   e) In the Bass Clef, Landmark Bass F is written on:

   line 4   or   line 5

   f) The notes in the Bass Clef are usually played with the:

   Left Hand   or   Right Hand

2. Draw a line connecting the Bass Clef notes to the keyboard (at the correct pitch).
   Name the notes. With your LH, play the notes and say the names of the notes out loud.

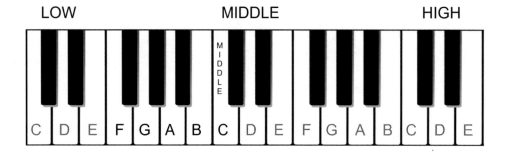

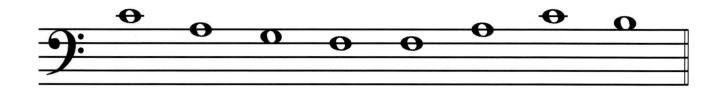

Lesson 3 Review Ultimate Sight Reading & Ear Training Games

1. PLAY "Stay in Shape". Beginning at the Start, name the pattern inside each Shape as: same line, same space, step up, step down, skip up or skip down.

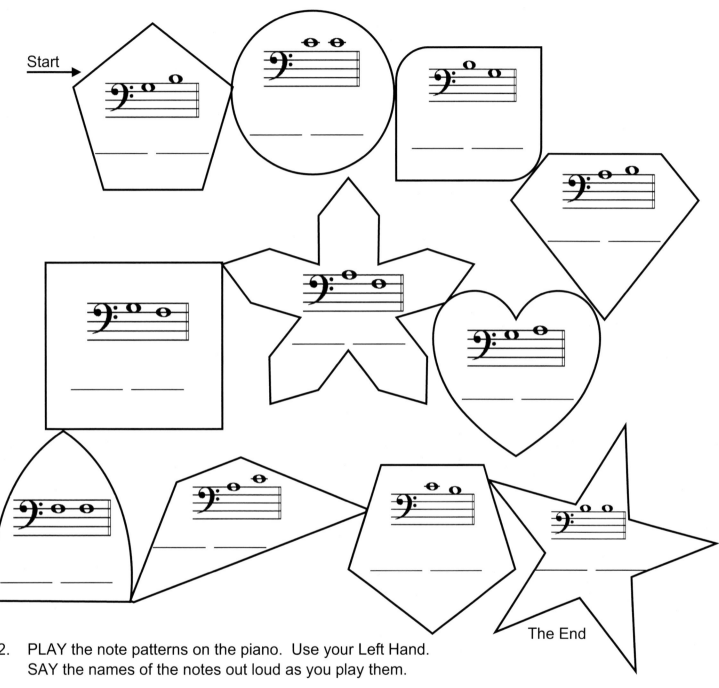

2. PLAY the note patterns on the piano. Use your Left Hand. SAY the names of the notes out loud as you play them.

Imagine, **C**ompose, **E**xplore!

Imagine So-La and Ti-Do are swimming!

Compose a song using the Bass Clef white keys F, G, A, B, C. Play them with your Left Hand.

Explore the sound as they swim down to the bottom of the pool and then back up to the top.

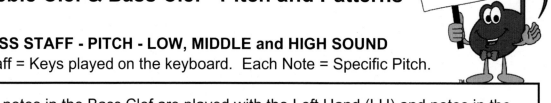

TREBLE STAFF & BASS STAFF - PITCH - LOW, MIDDLE and HIGH SOUND
Notes written on the staff = Keys played on the keyboard. Each Note = Specific Pitch.

So-La Says: Usually, notes in the Bass Clef are played with the Left Hand (LH) and notes in the Treble Clef are played with the Right Hand (RH). Middle C is in both the Bass Clef and Treble Clef.

Middle C in the Bass Clef is played with the LH. Middle C in the Treble Clef is played with the RH.

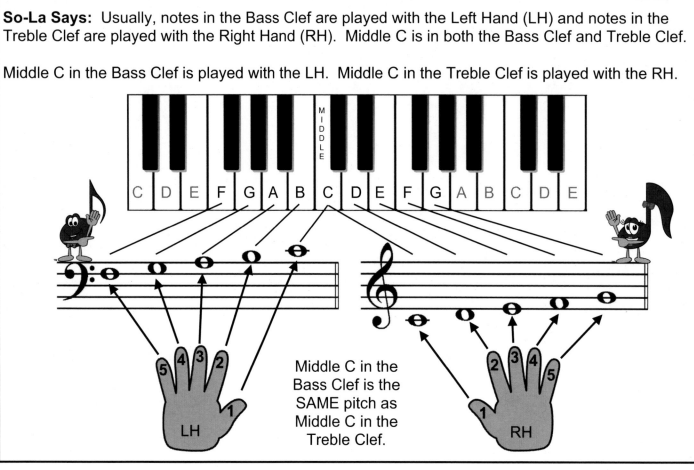

Middle C in the Bass Clef is the SAME pitch as Middle C in the Treble Clef.

1. Middle C in the Bass Clef is the _____ pitch as Middle C in the Treble Clef.

2. Name the notes on each staff. Draw a line connecting the notes on the staff to the keyboard (at the correct pitch). Name the key directly on the keyboard.

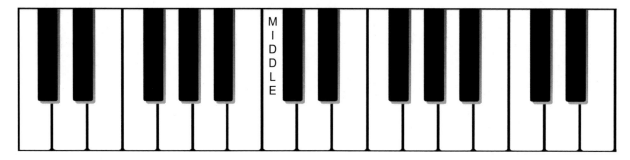

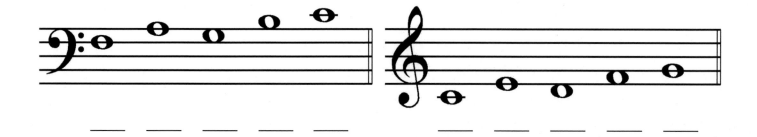

PITCH, CLEF and FINGER NUMBERS

On the Keyboard, the LOW sound and MIDDLE sound may be played with the Left Hand (LH).
On the Keyboard, the MIDDLE sound and HIGH sound may be played with the Right Hand (RH).

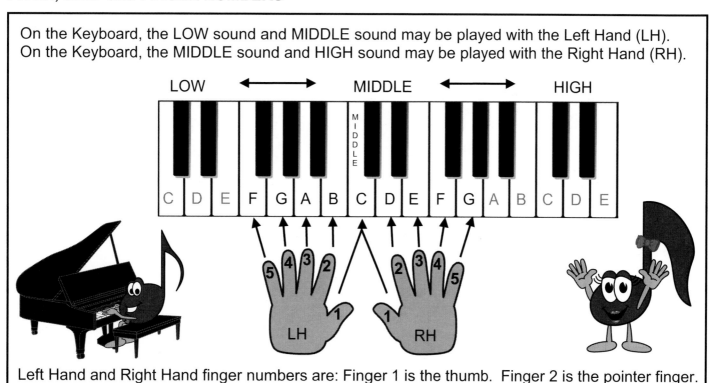

Left Hand and Right Hand finger numbers are: Finger 1 is the thumb. Finger 2 is the pointer finger.
Finger 3 is the tall finger. Finger 4 is the ring finger. Finger 5 is the baby finger.

♫ **Ti-Do Tip:** Middle C in the Bass Clef can be played with the Left Hand finger 1.
Middle C in the Treble Clef can be played with the Right Hand finger 1.

1. Write LH on the Left Hand. Write RH on the Right Hand. Names the keys directly on the keyboard.

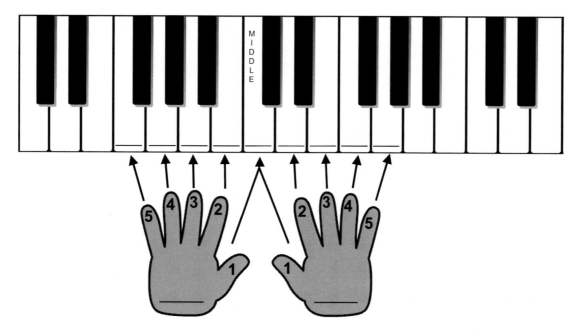

2. When both finger 1s (both thumbs) play Middle C on the keyboard, name the following white keys:

   a) The Left Hand finger 2 plays _____. The Right Hand finger 2 plays _____.

   b) The Left Hand finger 3 plays _____. The Right Hand finger 3 plays _____.

   c) The Left Hand finger 4 plays _____. The Right Hand finger 4 plays _____.

   d) The Left Hand finger 5 plays _____. The Right Hand finger 5 plays _____.

PATTERNS - STEP UP HIGH and STEP DOWN LOW

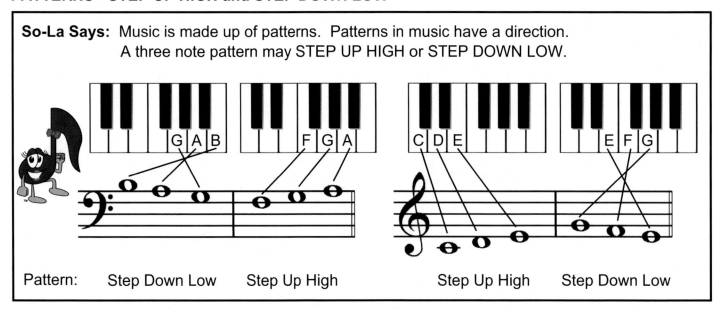

So-La Says: Music is made up of patterns. Patterns in music have a direction.
A three note pattern may STEP UP HIGH or STEP DOWN LOW.

Pattern: Step Down Low   Step Up High   Step Up High   Step Down Low

♫ **Ti-Do Tip:** A Step Up High Pattern or a Step Down Low Pattern will have 3 notes moving by step in the same direction (line note, space note, line note OR space note, line note, space note).

1. Name the notes in each clef. Circle the correct pattern: step up high or step down low.
   Play (on the piano) each pattern. Sing the pattern of the notes while you play.

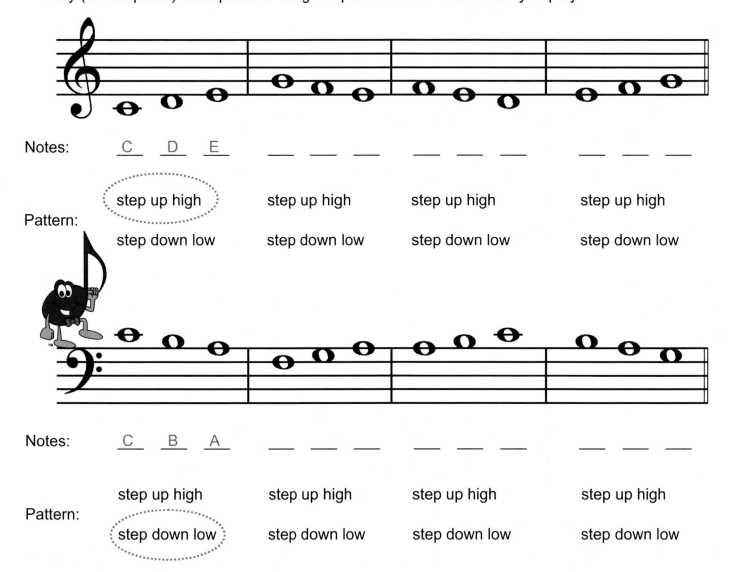

Notes: C   D   E   __   __   __   __   __   __   __   __   __

Pattern: (step up high)   step up high   step up high   step up high

            step down low   step down low   step down low   step down low

Notes: C   B   A   __   __   __   __   __   __   __   __   __

Pattern: step up high   step up high   step up high   step up high

            (step down low)   step down low   step down low   step down low

PATTERNS - SKIP UP HIGH and SKIP DOWN LOW

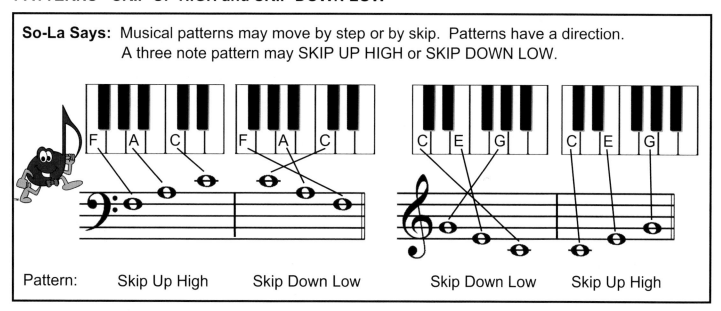

So-La Says: Musical patterns may move by step or by skip. Patterns have a direction.
A three note pattern may SKIP UP HIGH or SKIP DOWN LOW.

| Pattern: | Skip Up High | Skip Down Low | Skip Down Low | Skip Up High |

♫ **Ti-Do Tip:** A Skip Up High Pattern or a Skip Down Low Pattern will have 3 notes moving by skip in the same direction (line note, line note, line note OR space note, space note, space note).

1. Name the notes in each clef. Circle the correct pattern: skip up high or skip down low.
   Play (on the piano) each pattern. Sing the pattern of the notes while you play.

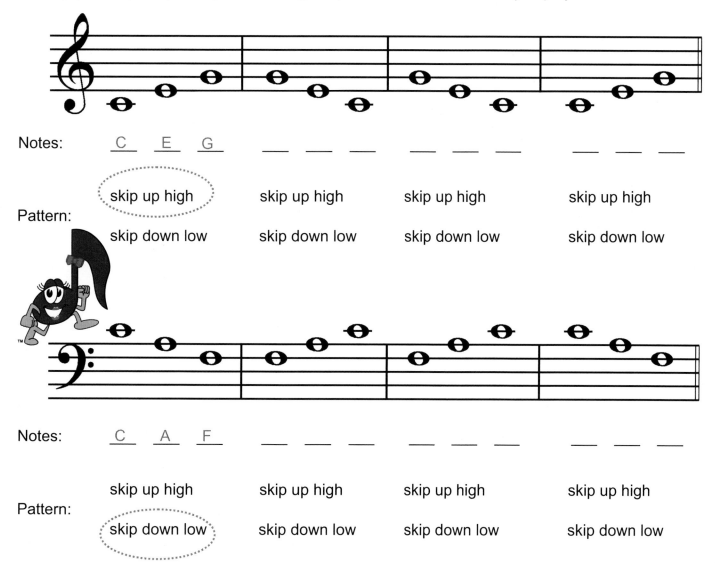

Notes: C E G   __ __ __   __ __ __   __ __ __

Pattern: (skip up high)   skip up high   skip up high   skip up high
          skip down low   skip down low   skip down low   skip down low

Notes: C A F   __ __ __   __ __ __   __ __ __

Pattern: skip up high   skip up high   skip up high   skip up high
          (skip down low) skip down low   skip down low   skip down low

Lesson 4 Review with So-La & Ti-Do

Check:

1. Write LH on the Left Hand. Write RH on the Right Hand. Name the keys directly on the keyboard.

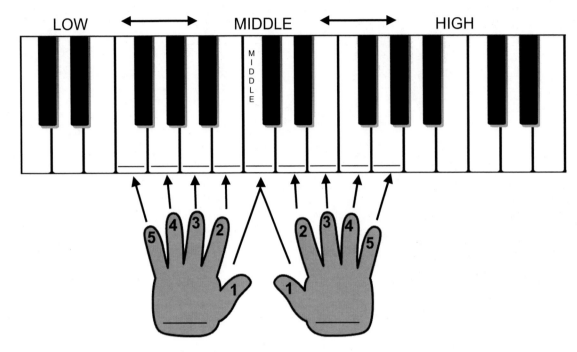

2. When both finger 1s (both thumbs) play Middle C on the keyboard, name the following notes:

   a) The Left Hand finger 2 plays _____. The Right Hand finger 2 plays _____.

   b) The Left Hand finger 4 plays _____. The Right Hand finger 4 plays _____.

   c) The Left Hand finger 1 plays _____. The Right Hand finger 1 plays _____.

   d) The Left Hand finger 3 plays _____. The Right Hand finger 3 plays _____.

   e) The Left Hand finger 5 plays _____. The Right Hand finger 5 plays _____.

3. Name the notes in each clef. Write the correct Finger Number below each note.
   Circle the correct pattern.
   Play (on the piano) each pattern. Sing the pattern of the notes while you play.

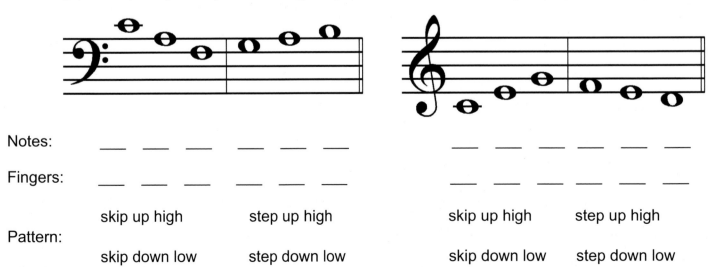

Notes: __ __ __ __ __ __   __ __ __ __ __ __

Fingers: __ __ __ __ __ __   __ __ __ __ __ __

Pattern:
    skip up high   step up high   skip up high   step up high

    skip down low   step down low   skip down low   step down low

Lesson 4 Review Ultimate Sight Reading & Ear Training Games

1. DRAW a line to connect the notes on the staff with the correct keys on the keyboard.
    WRITE the missing note names and finger numbers below each staff.

Middle C in the Bass Clef is the SAME pitch as Middle C in the Treble Clef.

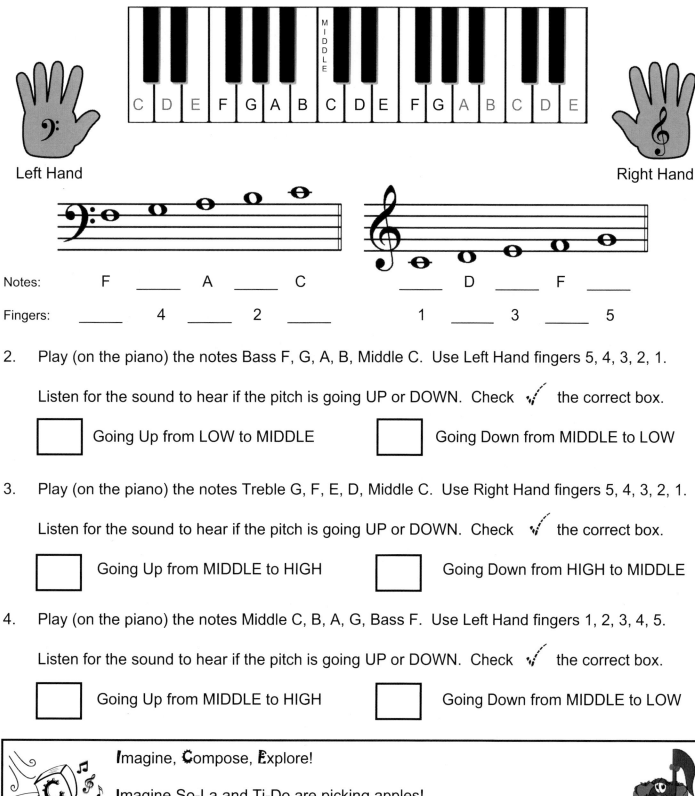

Left Hand   Right Hand

Notes: F _____ A _____ C   _____ D _____ F _____

Fingers: _____ 4 _____ 2 _____   1 _____ 3 _____ 5

2. Play (on the piano) the notes Bass F, G, A, B, Middle C. Use Left Hand fingers 5, 4, 3, 2, 1.

    Listen for the sound to hear if the pitch is going UP or DOWN. Check ✓ the correct box.

    ☐ Going Up from LOW to MIDDLE   ☐ Going Down from MIDDLE to LOW

3. Play (on the piano) the notes Treble G, F, E, D, Middle C. Use Right Hand fingers 5, 4, 3, 2, 1.

    Listen for the sound to hear if the pitch is going UP or DOWN. Check ✓ the correct box.

    ☐ Going Up from MIDDLE to HIGH   ☐ Going Down from HIGH to MIDDLE

4. Play (on the piano) the notes Middle C, B, A, G, Bass F. Use Left Hand fingers 1, 2, 3, 4, 5.

    Listen for the sound to hear if the pitch is going UP or DOWN. Check ✓ the correct box.

    ☐ Going Up from MIDDLE to HIGH   ☐ Going Down from MIDDLE to LOW

*I*magine, *C*ompose, *E*xplore!

*I*magine So-La and Ti-Do are picking apples!

*C*ompose a song - use your Left Hand to pick notes in the Bass Clef
and use your Right Hand to pick notes in the Treble Clef.

*E*xplore the sound as So-La and Ti-Do climb up the tree and drop apples to the ground.

Lesson 5   Quarter Notes, Whole Notes and Patterns

TYPES OF NOTES - QUARTER NOTE ♩ or ♪ **and WHOLE NOTE** ○

Different TYPES of notes have different NOTE VALUES - specific number of beats.
A beat is the length of sound (long or short). 1 scoop = 1 beat

Type of note: Quarter Note ♩ = 1 Beat (Note Value)   ♩ ♩ ♩ ♩ = 4 Beats
A quarter note sounds for 1 beat. A quarter note has 1 scoop.

Type of note: Whole Note ○ = 4 Beats (Note Value)   ○ = 4 Beats
A whole note sounds for 4 beats. A whole note has 4 scoops connected.

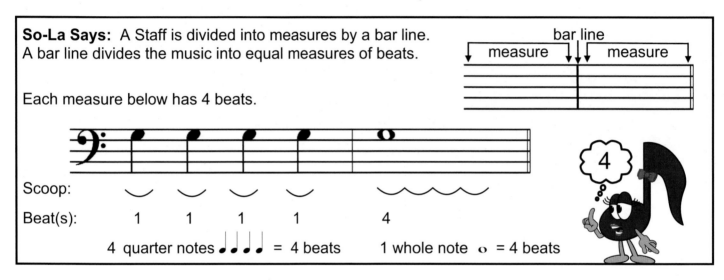

So-La Says: A Staff is divided into measures by a bar line.
A bar line divides the music into equal measures of beats.

Each measure below has 4 beats.

Scoop:	⌣	⌣	⌣	⌣	⌣⌣⌣
Beat(s):	1	1	1	1	4

4 quarter notes ♩♩♩♩ = 4 beats   1 whole note ○ = 4 beats

1. Name the notes. Write the number of beats for each note. Play the notes on the piano and say the patterns: step (up, up high or down, down low) or skip (up, up high or down, down low).

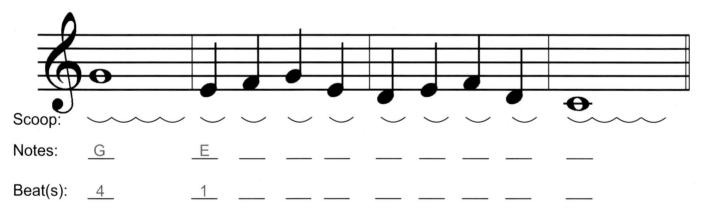

Scoop:									
Notes:	G	E	__	__	__	__	__	__	__
Beat(s):	4	1	__	__	__	__	__	__	__

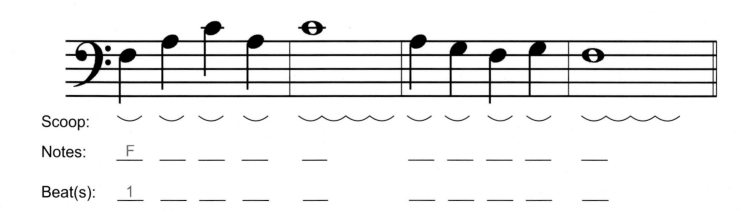

Scoop:									
Notes:	F	__	__	__	__	__	__	__	__
Beat(s):	1	__	__	__	__	__	__	__	__

QUARTER NOTE STEM DIRECTION - UP ON THE RIGHT and DOWN ON THE LEFT

So-La Says: A Quarter Note has a circle (oval shape) called a notehead. The notehead is colored in black. A Quarter Note has a line drawn on the side of the notehead called a stem.

As drawn by hand:
Notehead Stem

As seen in music:
Treble Clef Middle C, D, E, F, G - Quarter Note Stem UP on the right.

As drawn by hand:
Stem Notehead

As seen in music:
Bass Clef F, G, A, B, Middle C - Quarter Note Stem DOWN on the left.

♫ **Ti-Do Tip:** A stem length (how long the stem is) crosses 3 lines and goes through 3 spaces.

1. Write a quarter note on line note G (line 2) in the Treble Clef using the following steps:

Draw a notehead on line note G.

Fill in the notehead color in black.

Add a stem UP on the right of the notehead.

Write a quarter note on line note G.

2. Write a quarter note on line note F (line 4) in the Bass Clef using the following steps:

Draw a notehead on line note F.

Fill in the notehead color in black.

Add a stem DOWN on the left of the notehead.

Write a quarter note on line note F.

3. Add the correct stem direction to the following noteheads to create quarter notes in the Bass Clef and the Treble Clef. Name the notes.

Stem up or stem down?

___ ___ ___ ___ ___ ___   ___ ___ ___ ___ ___ ___

READING and WRITING SAME, STEP, SKIP PATTERNS - QUARTER NOTES

Music has Pitch (low, middle and high sounds). Music has Rhythm (short "Quarter Note" sounds and long "Whole Note" sounds). Music is Pitch and Rhythm written as Patterns of Notes.

So-La Says: Music is a Pattern (same, step, skip) that moves in a Direction (same, up, down). Music is written as Distances, the movement of notes on the staff from one note to the very next.

Pattern: Direction + Distance (movement) from one note to the very next note on the staff.

Same: Same note = line note to the same line note or space note to the same space note.

Step: Up or Down = line note to the next space note or space note to the next line note.

Skip: Up or Down = line note to the next line note (skipping a space) or space note to the next space note (skipping a line).

Notes:	G	G	E	D	D	F	E	C
Pattern:	same	skip	step	same	skip	step	skip	
	line	down	down	space	up	down	down	

---

1. Following the Pattern (Direction + Distance), add the missing notes. Use quarter notes. Write the missing note names. Play the melodies on the piano.

Notes:	C	___	E	G	___	E	___	C
Pattern:	skip	same	skip	step	step	step	step	
	up	line	up	down	down	down	down	

Notes:	F	___	A	___	A	___	B	___
Pattern:	same	skip	step	step	skip	step	step	
	line	up	down	up	up	down	up	

READING and WRITING SAME, STEP, SKIP PATTERNS - QUARTER NOTES & WHOLE NOTES

Music may be written using different Patterns (same, step, skip), Direction (same, up, down) and Rhythm (different note values) using Quarter Notes and Whole Notes.

So-La Says: Music may use Patterns with different types of notes that have different note values.

A Pattern (same, step, skip) may use a combination of quarter notes ♩ and/or whole notes o.

Pattern: Direction + Distance (movement) from one note to the very next note on the staff.

Patterns (Direction + Distance) are written in the Treble Clef and in the Bass Clef.

Patterns: Same Line or Same Space = line to same line or space to same space.
Step Up or Step Down = line to space or space to line.
Skip Up or Skip Down = line to line (skipping a space) or space to space (skipping a line).

Notes:	C	A	G	G	A	C	C	A	G	F
Pattern:	skip down	step down	same space	step up	skip up	same line	skip down	step down	step down	

---

1. Name the notes. Following the Pattern (Direction + Distance), add the missing notes.
   Use whole notes. Write the missing note names. Play the melodies on the piano.

Notes: ___ ___ ___ ___ ___ ___ ___

Pattern:	step down	step up	skip down	step up	skip down	step down

Notes: ___ ___ ___ ___ ___ ___ ___ ___ ___

Pattern:	step down	step down	skip up	skip up	skip down	same line	step down	same space	step down

Lesson 5 Review with So-La & Ti-Do

Check:

1. Circle the correct answer to complete each pattern.

    a) A Step moving up or down is a note written from:

    a space to a line   or   a space to a space (skipping a line).

    b) A Skip moving up or down is a note written from:

    a space to a line   or   a space to a space (skipping a line).

    c) A Step moving up or down is a note written from:

    a line to a space   or   a line to a line (skipping a space).

    d) A Skip moving up or down is a note written from:

    a line to a space   or   a line to a line (skipping a space).

2. Following the Pattern (Direction + Distance), add the missing notes. Use quarter notes.
    Write the missing note names. Play the melodies on the piano.

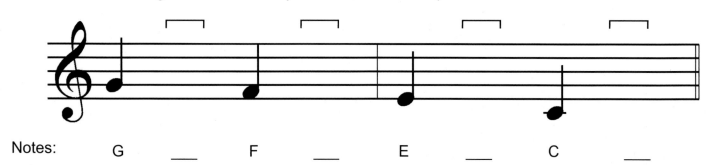

Notes: G ___ F ___ E ___ C ___

Pattern: same   step   same   step   same   skip   same
           line   down   space down   line   down   line

Notes: C ___ B ___ A ___ G ___

Pattern: same   step   same   step   skip   step   same
           line   down   space down   down   up   space

Imagine, **C**ompose, **E**xplore!

Imagine So-La and Ti-Do are in Outer Space!

Compose a song about your "Outer Space Adventure" with So-La & Ti-Do.

Explore the different sound of each Pattern: same, step (up or down) or skip (up or down).

1. COMPOSE a song by adding the missing note at the end of each melody. Pick a Pattern from a Star. Use a whole note. Name the notes. Play your melody on the piano.

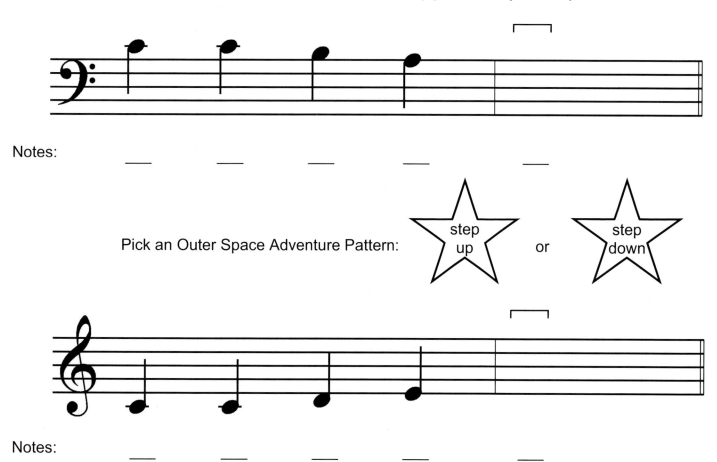

Notes: ___ ___ ___ ___ ___

Pick an Outer Space Adventure Pattern: **step up** or **step down**

Notes: ___ ___ ___ ___ ___

Pick an Outer Space Adventure Pattern: **skip up** or **skip down**

 Are you ready to go into Outer Space?

Before you play, SAY the Patterns (Direction and Distance) between the notes.

Starting at the first note (C), point to the music and SAY (identify) each Pattern as: same line, same space, step up, step down, skip up or skip down.

PLAY each Outer Space Adventure on the Piano.

Lesson 6   Treble Clef - Landmark Notes

Treble Clef: Middle C - Ledger Line, Treble G - Line 2, Treble C - Space 3

Landmark Note Middle C is written below the Treble Staff on a ledger line.
Landmark Note Treble G is written on the "**G**" line, line 2.

Landmark Note Treble C is written in space 3. **Space number 3 - That's Treble C.**

As seen in music:

As drawn by hand:

← Treble C space 3 →
← Treble G line 2 →
← Middle C ledger line →

C   G   C   C   G   C

1. Fill in the blanks.

   a) Landmark Note Middle C is written below the Treble Staff on a _____ line.

   b) Landmark Note Treble G is written on the "G" line, line number _____.

   c) Landmark Note Treble C is written in a space, space number _____ - That's Treble C.

♫ **Ti-Do Tip:** Always use a ruler to draw a straight ledger line below the Treble Staff for Middle C.

2. On each staff, draw a Treble Clef. Write the landmark notes Middle C, Treble G and Treble C. Use whole notes. Draw a line connecting the notes to the keyboard (at the correct pitch). Name the notes.

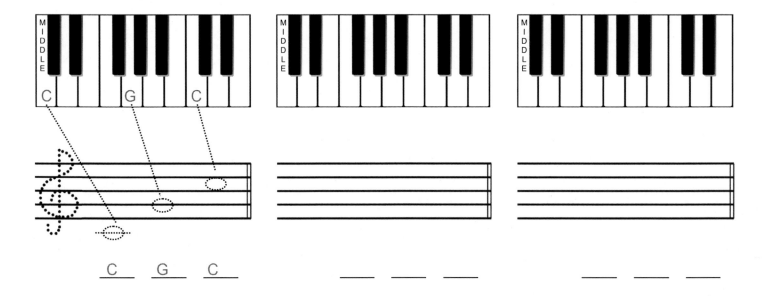

C   G   C   ___ ___ ___   ___ ___ ___

TREBLE CLEF - PATTERNS FROM LANDMARK NOTES

On the Treble Staff, movement between landmark notes Middle C, Treble G and Treble C may move by steps (up or down) or move by skips (up or down). A landmark note may also be repeated (same).

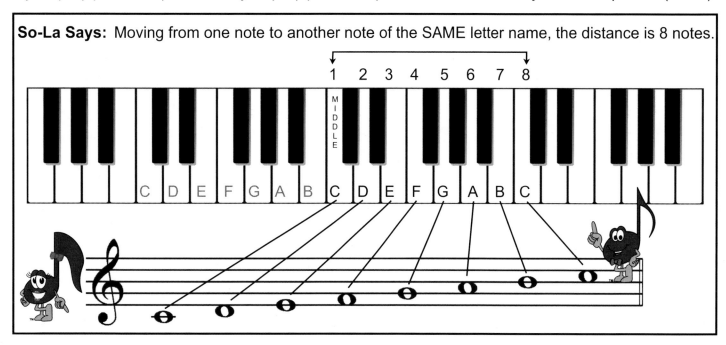

So-La Says: Moving from one note to another note of the SAME letter name, the distance is 8 notes.

1. Moving from Middle C to Treble C (C, D, E, F, G, A, B, C), the distance is _____ notes.

2. Following the Pattern, add the missing notes. Use whole notes. Name the missing notes.

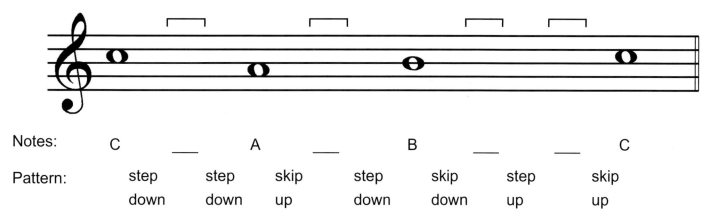

Notes:	C	___	A	___	B	___	___	C
Pattern:	step down	step down	skip up	step down	skip down	step up	skip up	

3. Name the notes. Draw a line connecting the notes to the keyboard (at the correct pitch).

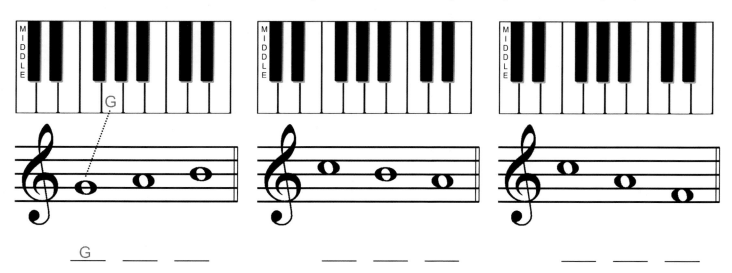

G   ___   ___   ___   ___   ___   ___   ___   ___

TREBLE CLEF - MIDDLE C UP to TREBLE C

In the Treble Clef, notes may move from a MIDDLE sound (pitch) UP to a HIGH sound (pitch).
Notes moving UP the staff from Middle C to Treble C (Space 3) become HIGHER in sound.

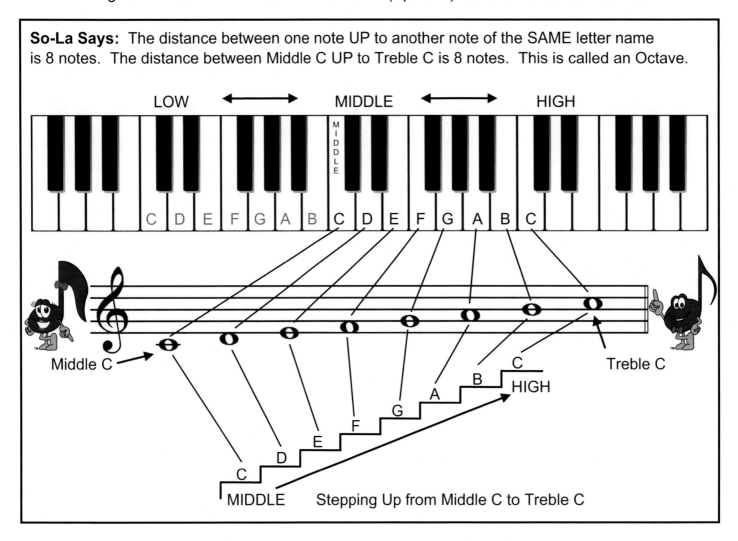

So-La Says: The distance between one note UP to another note of the SAME letter name is 8 notes. The distance between Middle C UP to Treble C is 8 notes. This is called an Octave.

1. Name the 8 notes (octave) from Middle C UP to Treble C. __C__ __D__ ___ ___ ___ ___ ___ ___

2. Draw a line connecting the Treble Clef notes to the keyboard (at the correct pitch). Name the notes.

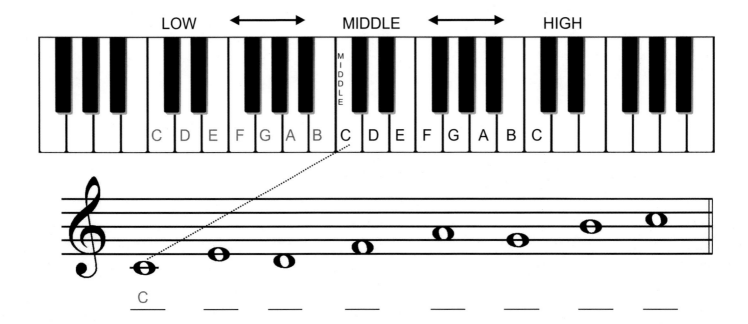

TREBLE CLEF - TREBLE C DOWN to MIDDLE C

In the Treble Clef, notes may move from a HIGH sound (pitch) DOWN to a MIDDLE sound (pitch).
Notes moving DOWN the staff from Treble C (Space 3) to Middle C become LOWER in sound.

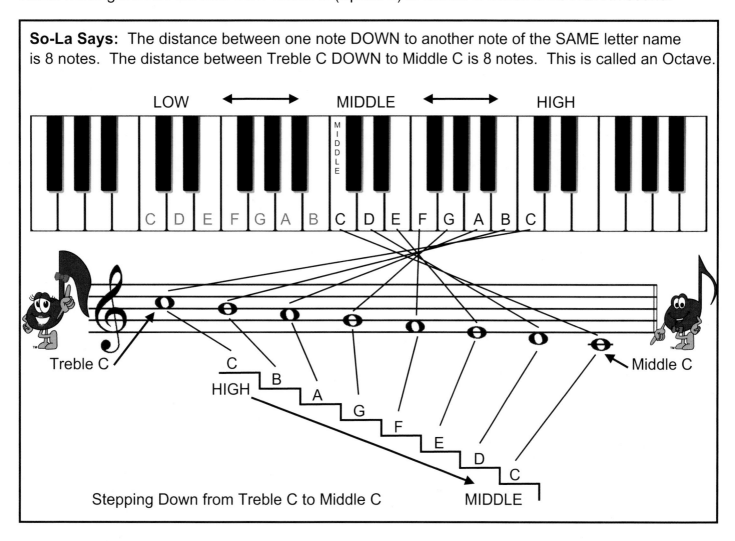

So-La Says: The distance between one note DOWN to another note of the SAME letter name is 8 notes. The distance between Treble C DOWN to Middle C is 8 notes. This is called an Octave.

Stepping Down from Treble C to Middle C

1. Name the 8 notes (octave) from Middle C DOWN to Treble C. _C_ _B_ __ __ __ __ __ __

2. Draw a line connecting the Treble Clef notes to the keyboard (at the correct pitch). Name the notes.

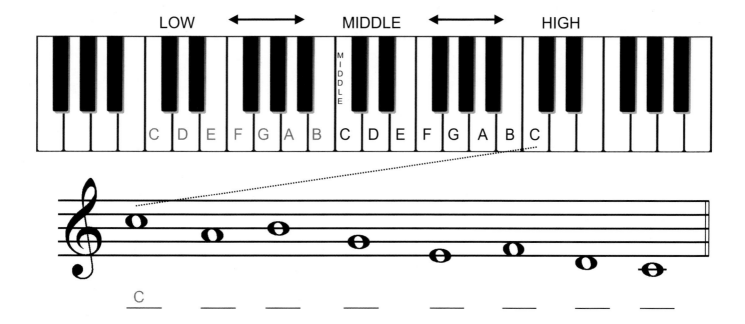

_C_ __ __ __ __ __ __ __

TREBLE CLEF - LINE NOTES

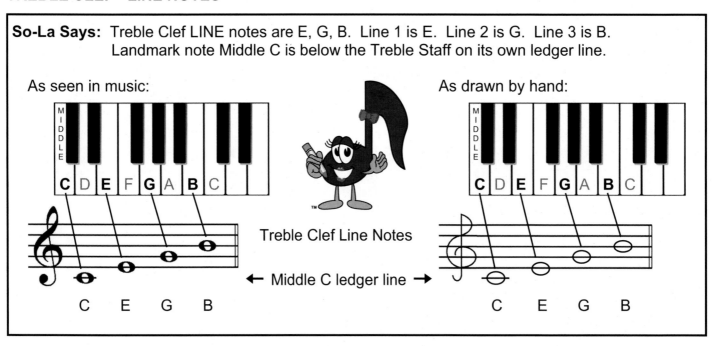

So-La Says: Treble Clef LINE notes are E, G, B. Line 1 is E. Line 2 is G. Line 3 is B. Landmark note Middle C is below the Treble Staff on its own ledger line.

As seen in music:

As drawn by hand:

Treble Clef Line Notes

← Middle C ledger line →

C E G B

C E G B

1. Name the Treble Clef line notes. Line 1 is _____. Line 2 is _____. Line 3 is _____.

2. The ledger line note below the Treble Staff is _____ _____.

3. Name the line notes. Draw a line connecting the notes to the keyboard (at the correct pitch).

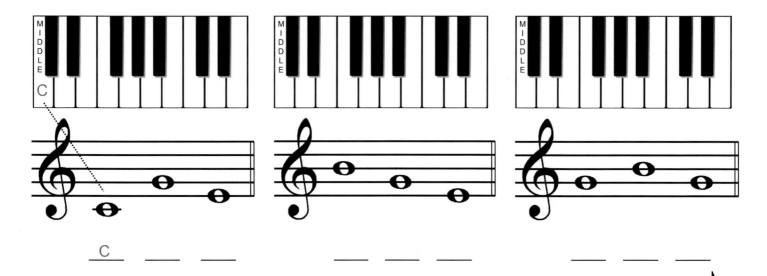

C ___ ___   ___ ___ ___   ___ ___ ___

4. On each staff, draw a Treble Clef. Write the following line notes. Use whole notes.

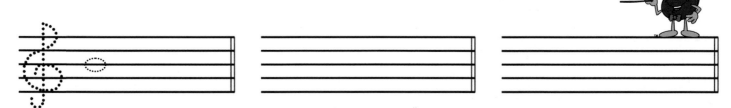

B   G   E   G   E   B   Middle C   B   G

TREBLE CLEF - SPACE NOTES

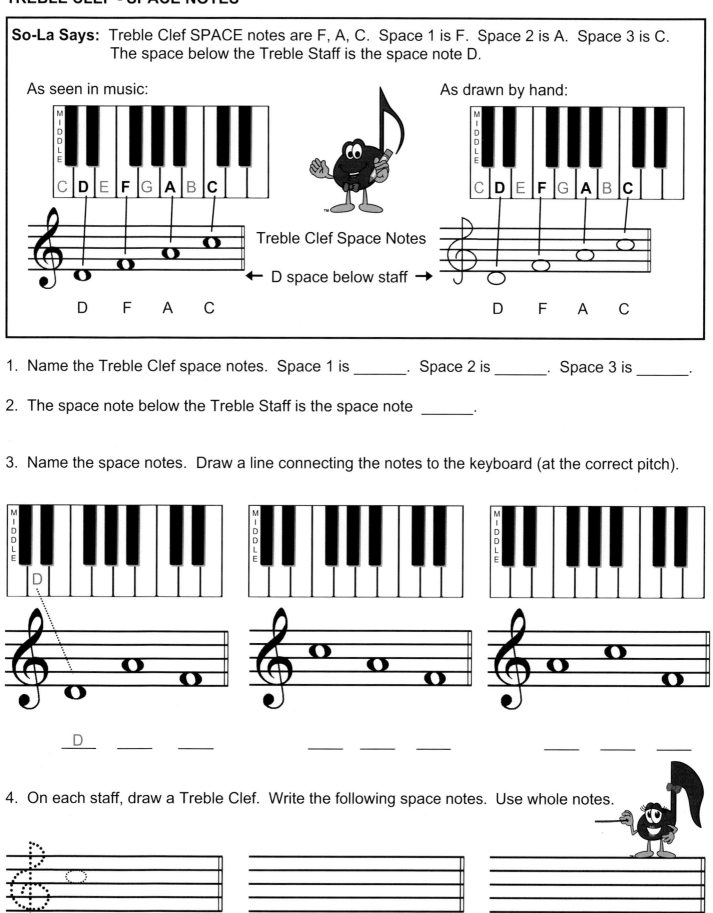

So-La Says: Treble Clef SPACE notes are F, A, C. Space 1 is F. Space 2 is A. Space 3 is C. The space below the Treble Staff is the space note D.

As seen in music:

As drawn by hand:

Treble Clef Space Notes

← D space below staff →

D   F   A   C

D   F   A   C

1. Name the Treble Clef space notes. Space 1 is _____. Space 2 is _____. Space 3 is _____.

2. The space note below the Treble Staff is the space note _____.

3. Name the space notes. Draw a line connecting the notes to the keyboard (at the correct pitch).

D

___D___   _____   _____   _____   _____   _____   _____   _____   _____

4. On each staff, draw a Treble Clef. Write the following space notes. Use whole notes.

C   A   F   F   A   C   D   C   A

Lesson 6 Review with So-La & Ti-Do

Check:

1. Name the following notes. Draw a line connecting the Treble Clef notes to the keyboard (at the correct pitch). Name the corresponding keys directly on the keyboard.

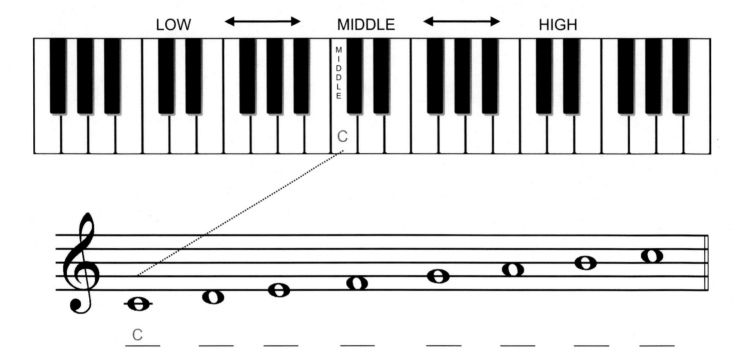

2. Name the Treble Clef notes for each line and space.

   a) The note in Space 3 of the Treble Staff is _____.

   b) The note on Line 3 of the Treble Staff is _____.

   c) The note in Space 2 of the Treble Staff is _____.

   d) The note on Line 2 of the Treble Staff is _____.

   e) The note in Space 1 of the Treble Staff is _____.

   f) The note on Line 1 of the Treble Staff is _____.

   g) The note in the space below the Treble Staff is _____.

   h) The note on the ledger line below the Treble Staff is _____.

Lesson 6 Review Ultimate Sight Reading & Ear Training Games

1.   So-La and Ti-Do are eating Ice Cream.

   a) PICK 2 different colors of crayons. WRITE the name of one color for each:

   Color: Line Note: _____.   Space Note: _____.

   b) COLOR the Ice Cream (line note or space note) with the color that you picked.

   c) NAME each note directly on the Ice Cream Cone.

C

2.   PLAY "Scoop the Ice Cream".

Your Teacher will play one of the notes from the Ice Cream Cones.

Look at the note that your Teacher is playing on the piano.

Point to the correct Ice Cream Cone Note.

Lesson 7   Bass Clef - Landmark Notes

Bass Clef: Bass C - Space 2, Bass F - Line 4, Middle C - Ledger Line

Landmark Note Middle C is written above the Bass Staff on a ledger line.
Landmark Note Bass F is written on the "F" line, line 4.

Landmark Note Bass C is written in space 2. **Space number 2 - That's Bass C.**

As seen in music: As drawn by hand:

← Middle C ledger line →
← Bass F line 4 →
← Bass C space 2 →

1. Fill in the blanks.

   a) Landmark Note Middle C is written above the Bass Staff on a _____ line.

   b) Landmark Note Bass F is written on the "F" line, line number _____.

   c) Landmark Note Bass C is written in a space, space number _____ - That's Bass C.

♫ **Ti-Do Tip:** Always use a ruler to draw a straight ledger line above the Bass Staff for Middle C.

2. On each staff, draw a Bass Clef. Write the landmark notes Bass C, Bass F and Middle C. Use whole notes. Draw a line connecting the notes to the keyboard (at the correct pitch). Name the notes.

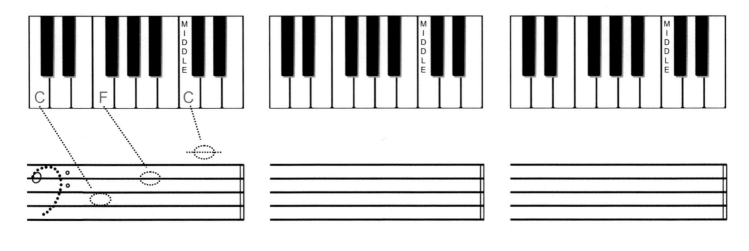

    C   F   C   ___ ___ ___   ___ ___ ___

BASS CLEF - PATTERNS FROM LANDMARK NOTES

On the Bass Staff, movement between landmark notes Bass C, Bass F and Middle C may move by steps (up or down) or move by skips (up or down). A landmark note may also be repeated (same).

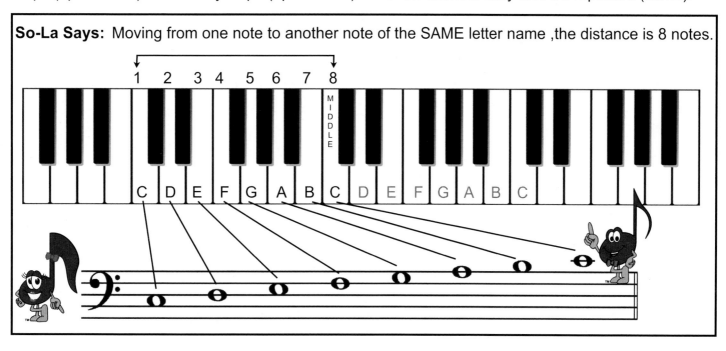

So-La Says: Moving from one note to another note of the SAME letter name ,the distance is 8 notes.

1. Moving from Bass C to Middle C (C, D, E, F, G, A, B, C), the distance is _____ notes.

2. Following the Pattern, add the missing notes. Use whole notes. Name the missing notes.

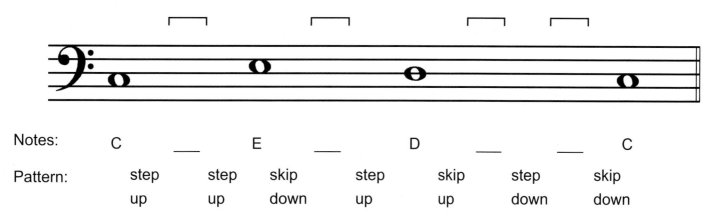

Notes:	C	___	E	___	D	___	___	C
Pattern:	step up	step up	skip down	step up	skip up	step down	skip down	

3. Name the notes. Draw a line connecting the notes to the keyboard (at the correct pitch).

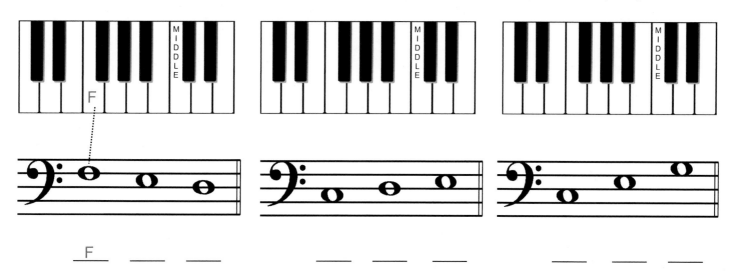

F ___ ___ ___   ___ ___ ___   ___ ___ ___

BASS CLEF - BASS C UP to MIDDLE C

In the Bass Clef, notes may move from a LOW sound (pitch) UP to a MIDDLE sound (pitch).
Notes moving UP the staff from Bass C (Space 2) to Middle C become HIGHER in sound.

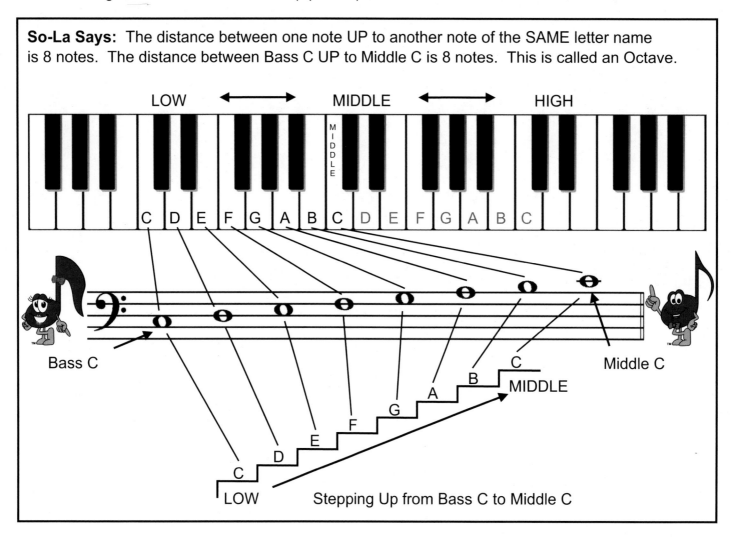

So-La Says: The distance between one note UP to another note of the SAME letter name is 8 notes. The distance between Bass C UP to Middle C is 8 notes. This is called an Octave.

Stepping Up from Bass C to Middle C

1. Name the 8 notes (octave) from Bass C UP to Middle C. <u>C</u> <u>D</u> ___ ___ ___ ___ ___ ___

2. Draw a line connecting the Bass Clef notes to the keyboard (at the correct pitch). Name the notes.

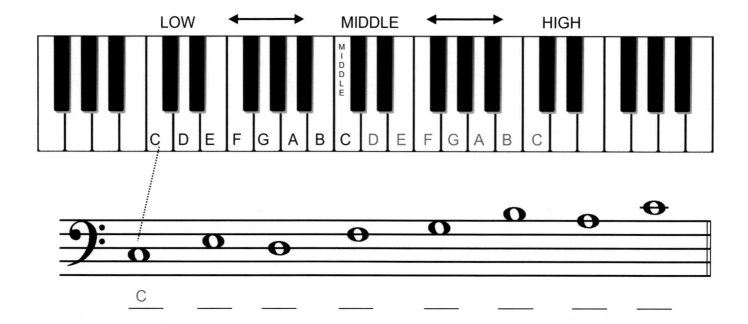

<u>C</u> ___ ___ ___ ___ ___ ___ ___

BASS CLEF - MIDDLE C DOWN to BASS C

In the Bass Clef, notes may move from a MIDDLE sound (pitch) DOWN to a LOW sound (pitch).
Notes moving DOWN the staff from Middle C to Bass C (Space 2) become LOWER in sound.

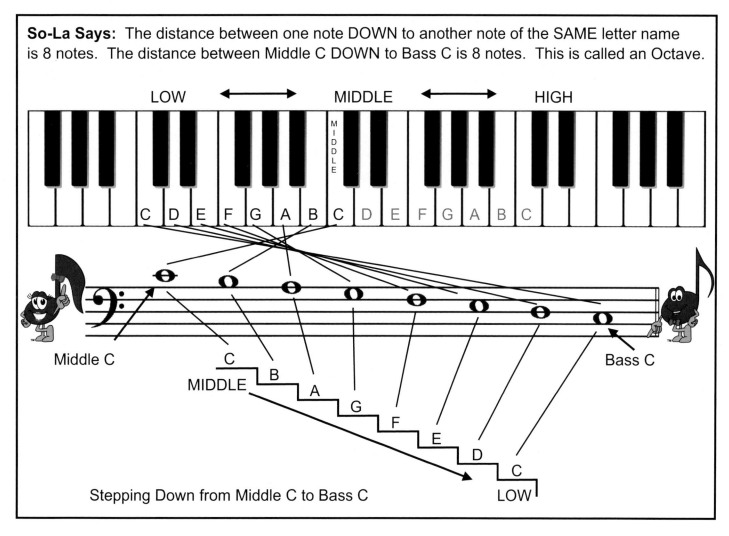

So-La Says: The distance between one note DOWN to another note of the SAME letter name
is 8 notes. The distance between Middle C DOWN to Bass C is 8 notes. This is called an Octave.

Stepping Down from Middle C to Bass C

1. Name the 8 notes (octave) from Middle C DOWN to Bass C. _C_ _B_ __ __ __ __ __ __

2. Draw a line connecting the Bass Clef notes to the keyboard (at the correct pitch). Name the notes.

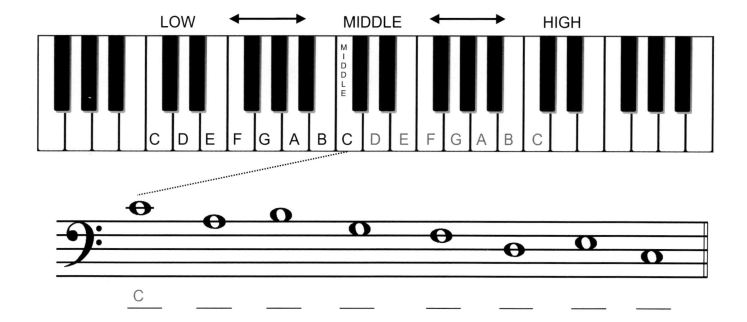

BASS CLEF - LINE NOTES

So-La Says: Bass Clef LINE notes are D, F, A. Line 3 is D. Line 2 is F. Line 1 is A.
Landmark note Middle C is above the Bass Staff on its own ledger line.

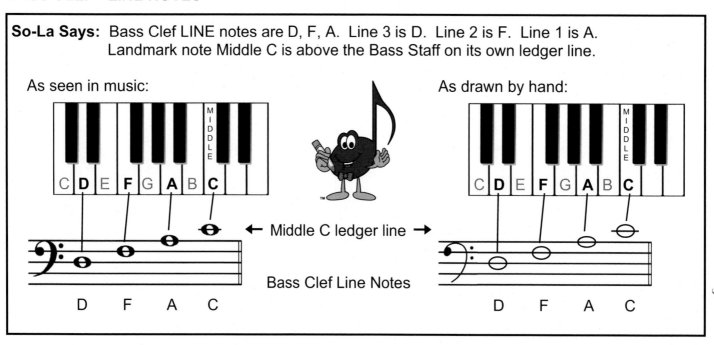

1. Name the Bass Clef line notes. Line 3 is _____. Line 2 is _____. Line 1 is _____.

2. The ledger line note above the Bass Staff is _____ _____.

3. Name the line notes. Draw a line connecting the notes to the keyboard (at the correct pitch).

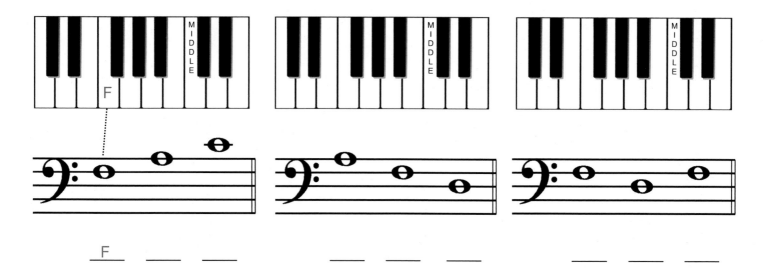

F

4. On each staff, draw a Bass Clef. Write the following line notes. Use whole notes.

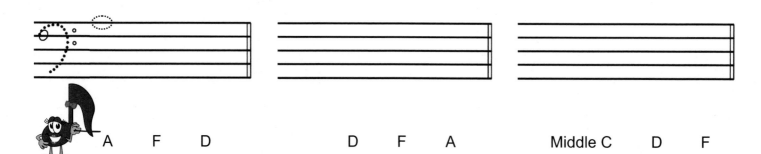

A   F   D   D   F   A   Middle C   D   F

BASS CLEF - SPACE NOTES

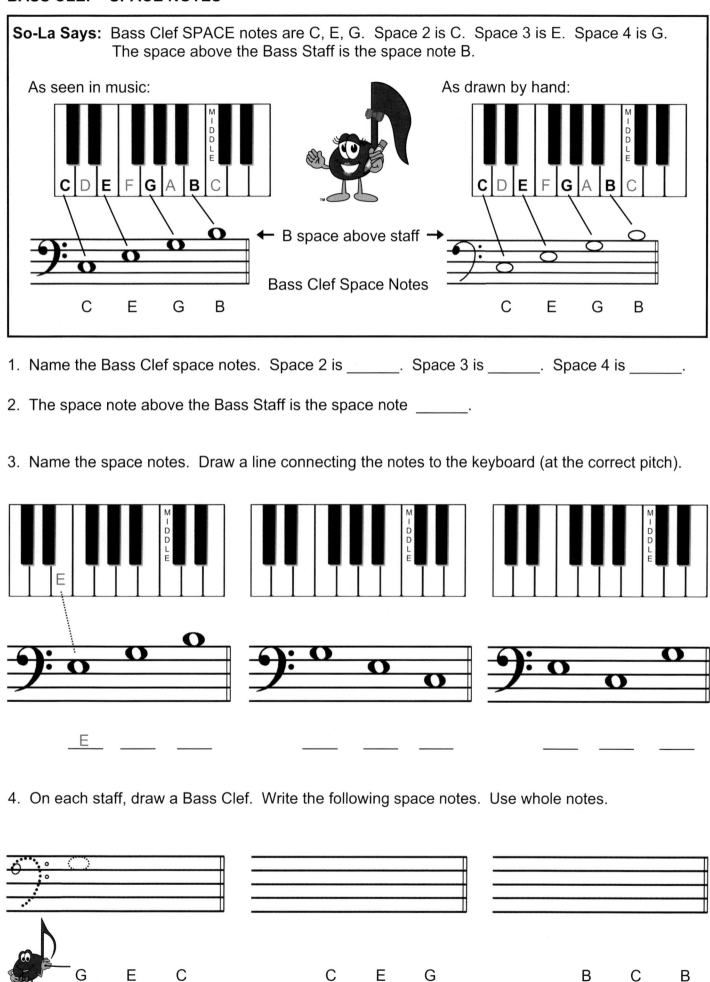

So-La Says: Bass Clef SPACE notes are C, E, G. Space 2 is C. Space 3 is E. Space 4 is G. The space above the Bass Staff is the space note B.

As seen in music:

As drawn by hand:

← B space above staff →

Bass Clef Space Notes

C   E   G   B

C   E   G   B

1. Name the Bass Clef space notes. Space 2 is _____. Space 3 is _____. Space 4 is _____.

2. The space note above the Bass Staff is the space note _____.

3. Name the space notes. Draw a line connecting the notes to the keyboard (at the correct pitch).

E

_E_ ____ ____ ____

____ ____ ____

____ ____ ____

4. On each staff, draw a Bass Clef. Write the following space notes. Use whole notes.

G   E   C

C   E   G

B   C   B

Lesson 7 Review with So-La & Ti-Do

Check:

1. Name the following notes. Draw a line connecting the Bass Clef notes to the keyboard (at the correct pitch). Name the corresponding keys directly on the keyboard.

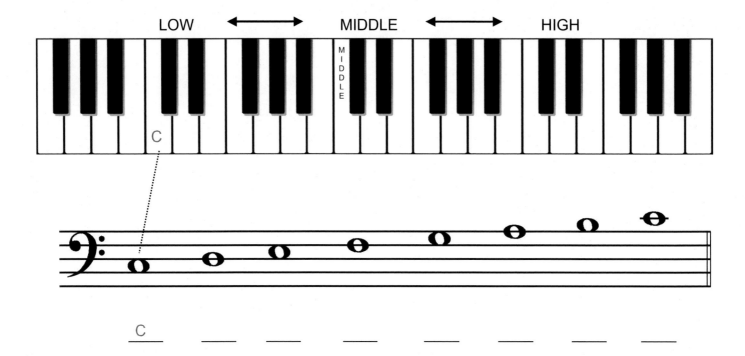

2. Name the Bass Clef notes for each line and space.

a) The note on the ledger line above the Bass Staff is _____.

b) The note in the space above the Bass Staff is _____.

c) The note on Line 5 of the Bass Staff is _____.

d) The note in Space 4 of the Bass Staff is _____.

e) The note on Line 4 of the Bass Staff is _____.

f) The note in Space 3 of the Bass Staff is _____.

g) The note on Line 3 of the Bass Staff is _____.

h) The note in Space 2 of the Bass Staff is _____.

Lesson 7 Review Ultimate Sight Reading & Ear Training Games

1.   So-La and Ti-Do have a Bright Idea.

  a) PICK 2 different colors of crayons. WRITE the name of one color for each:

  Color: Line Note: _____.   Space Note: _____.

  b) COLOR the Light Bulb (line note or space note) with the color that you picked.

  c) NAME each note directly on the Light Bulb.

2.   PLAY "Turn on the Light Bulb".

Your Teacher will play one of the notes from the Light Bulbs.

Look at the note that your Teacher is playing on the piano.

Point to the correct Light Bulb Note.

TREBLE CLEF PATTERNS - SAME LINE, SAME SPACE, STEP UP, SKIP UP

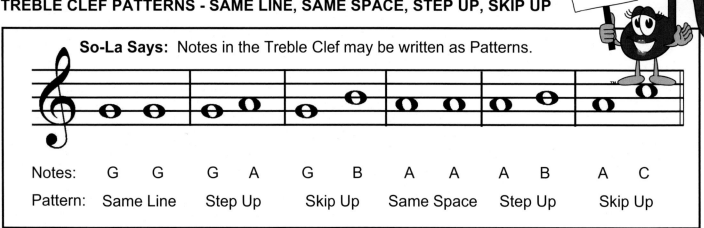

So-La Says: Notes in the Treble Clef may be written as Patterns.

Notes:	G	G	G	A	G	B	A	A	A	B	A	C
Pattern:	Same Line		Step Up		Skip Up		Same Space		Step Up		Skip Up	

1. Name the notes. Name the Pattern as: same line, same space, step up or skip up.

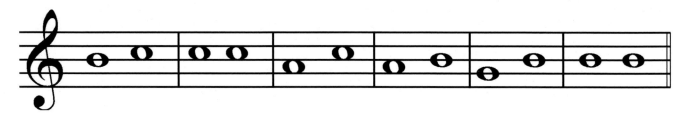

Notes: <u>B</u>   <u>C</u>   ___ ___   ___ ___   ___ ___   ___ ___   ___ ___

Pattern: <u>step</u>   _____   _____   _____   _____   _____

           <u>up</u>   _____   _____   _____   _____   _____

2. Name the notes in the Treble Clef.

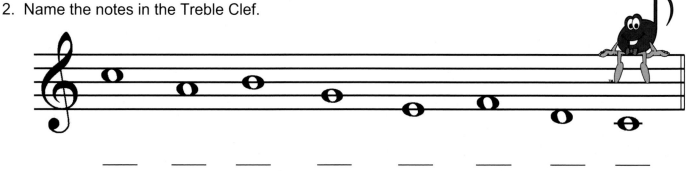

___   ___   ___   ___   ___   ___   ___   ___

3. Draw a Treble Clef on the staff. Write the following notes. Use whole notes.
   Use a ruler to draw a ledger line below the Treble Staff when writing the line note Middle C.

         Middle C   E   F   A   Treble C   B   G

TREBLE CLEF PATTERNS - SAME LINE, SAME SPACE, STEP DOWN, SKIP DOWN

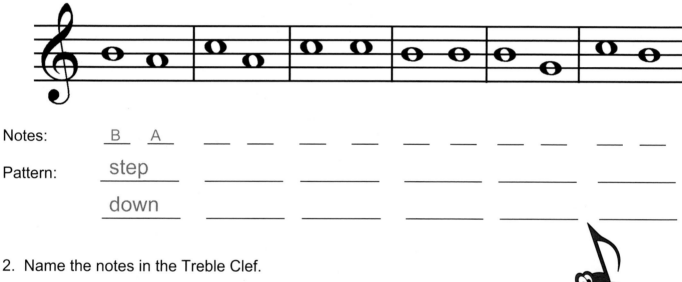

So-La Says: Notes in the Treble Clef may be written as Patterns that begin on a line note or a space note.

Notes:	B	B	B	A	B	G	C	C	C	B	C	A
Pattern:	Same Line		Step Down		Skip Down		Same Space		Step Down		Skip Down	

1. Name the notes. Name the Pattern as: same line, same space, step down or skip down.

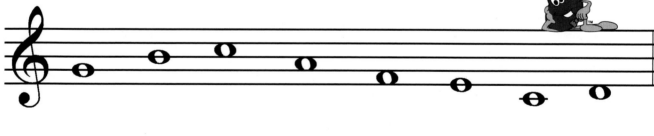

Notes: <u>B</u> <u>A</u> __ __ __ __ __ __ __ __ __ __

Pattern: <u>step</u> _____ _____ _____ _____ _____

<u>down</u> _____ _____ _____ _____ _____

2. Name the notes in the Treble Clef.

_____ _____ _____ _____ _____ _____ _____

3. Draw a Treble Clef on the staff. Write the following notes. Use whole notes.
   Use a ruler to draw a ledger line below the Treble Staff when writing the line note Middle C.

Treble C   B   G   A   F   D   Middle C

TREBLE CLEF - STEP UP HIGH and SKIP UP HIGH

So-La Says: Music may move in different Patterns of step up high or skip up high. Patterns may be connected by repeating the same note, or by a step (up or down) or by a skip (up or down).

step up
C   D   E   F   A   C
step up high   skip up high

skip down
C   E   G   E   F   G
skip up high   step up high

1. Patterns: C, D, E is a _____ up high Pattern. F, A, C is a _____ up high Pattern.

C, E, G is a _____ up high Pattern. E, F, G is a _____ up high Pattern.

2. Following the Pattern, add the missing notes. Use whole notes. Name the missing notes.

Notes: D   ___   ___   E   ___   ___   G   ___   ___   A   ___   ___

Pattern: step up high   skip up high   step up high   step up high

3. Name the notes. Draw a line connecting the notes to the keyboard (at the correct pitch).
   Name the Pattern as step up high or skip up high.

Notes: ____   ____   ____   ____   ____   ____   ____   ____   ____

Pattern: _____ up high   _____ up high   _____ up high

TREBLE CLEF - STEP DOWN LOW and SKIP DOWN LOW

So-La Says: Music may move in different Patterns of step down low or skip down low. Patterns may be connected by repeating the same note, or by a step (up or down) or by a skip (up or down).

same line
B A G   G E C
step down low   skip down low

same space
C A F   F E D
skip down low   step down low

1. Patterns: B, A, G is a _____ down low Pattern. G, E, C is a _____ down low Pattern.

   C, A, F is a _____ down low Pattern. F, E, D is a _____ down low Pattern.

2. Following the Pattern, add the missing notes. Use whole notes. Name the missing notes.

Notes: C ___ ___   C ___ ___   A ___ ___   E ___ ___

Pattern: step down low   skip down low   skip down low   step down low

3. Name the notes. Draw a line connecting the notes to the keyboard (at the correct pitch).
   Name the Pattern as step down low or skip down low.

Notes: ___ ___ ___   ___ ___ ___   ___ ___ ___

Pattern: _____ down low   _____ down low   _____ down low

TREBLE CLEF - C MAJOR PENTASCALE PATTERN - MAJOR (HAPPY) SOUND

So-La Says: A 5 note pattern moving by step (up or down) is called a Pentascale. Penta means 5.
A PENTASCALE is 5 notes moving by step in the same direction (up or down).

C pentascale - C, D, E, F, G or G, F, E, D, C - has a HAPPY sound called a MAJOR sound.

C Major pentascale may be written using Quarter Notes ♩ and Whole Notes o.

Notes:	C	D	E	F	G		G	F	E	D	C
Pattern:	C	step	up	high	G		G	step	down	low	C

1. A 5 note pattern moving by step (up or down) is called a _____. Penta means ___.

2. C Major pentascale has a happy sound called a _____ sound.

3. Name the notes. Following the pentascale pattern, add the missing notes. Use quarter notes.
   Write the missing note names. Play the C Major pentascale patterns on the piano.

Notes: __ __ __ __ __   __ __ __ __ __

Pattern:	C	step	up	high	G		G	step	down	low	C

4. Draw a line connecting the notes to the keyboard (at the correct pitch). Name the C Major
   pentascale pattern as stepping up or stepping down.

C Major pentascale - stepping _____   C Major pentascale - stepping _____

So-La Says: A pentascale is a 5 note pattern moving by step in the same direction (up or down). A PENTASCALE may have a MAJOR (happy) sound or a MINOR (sad) sound.

D pentascale - D, E, F, G, A or A, G, F, E, D - has a SAD sound called a MINOR sound.

D minor pentascale may be written using Quarter Notes ♩ and Whole Notes 𝅝.

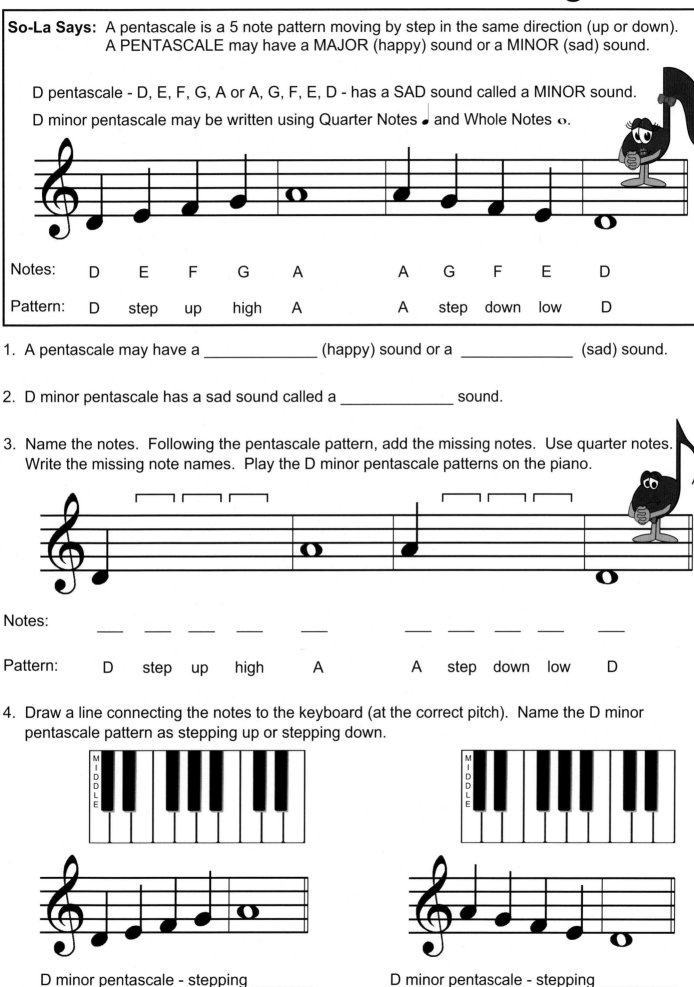

Notes:	D	E	F	G	A		A	G	F	E	D
Pattern:	D	step	up	high	A		A	step	down	low	D

1. A pentascale may have a _____ (happy) sound or a _____ (sad) sound.

2. D minor pentascale has a sad sound called a _____ sound.

3. Name the notes. Following the pentascale pattern, add the missing notes. Use quarter notes. Write the missing note names. Play the D minor pentascale patterns on the piano.

Notes: __ __ __ __ __   __ __ __ __ __

Pattern:	D	step	up	high	A		A	step	down	low	D

4. Draw a line connecting the notes to the keyboard (at the correct pitch). Name the D minor pentascale pattern as stepping up or stepping down.

D minor pentascale - stepping _____   D minor pentascale - stepping _____

Lesson 8 Review with So-La & Ti-Do

Check:

1. Fill in the blank to complete each sentence.

    a) A pentascale is a _____ note pattern moving by step in the same direction (up or down).

    b) C Major pentascale has a _____ sound called a Major sound.

    c) D minor pentascale has a _____ sound called a minor sound.

2. When written in the Treble Clef, the C Major pentascale and the D minor pentascale are usually played with the Right Hand.

    a) Draw a line connecting the notes to the keyboard (at the correct pitch). Name the keys directly on the keyboard.

C Major pentascale

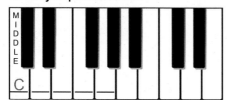

D minor pentascale

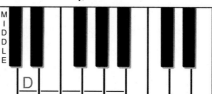

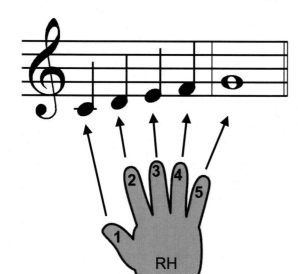

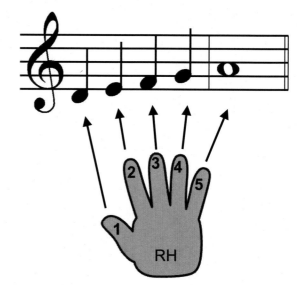

    b) Write the note name for each Finger Number.

When playing the C Major pentascale:

The Right Hand finger 1 plays ___C___.
The Right Hand finger 2 plays _____.
The Right Hand finger 3 plays _____.
The Right Hand finger 4 plays _____.
The Right Hand finger 5 plays _____.

When playing the D minor pentascale:

The Right Hand finger 1 plays ___D___.
The Right Hand finger 2 plays _____.
The Right Hand finger 3 plays _____.
The Right Hand finger 4 plays _____.
The Right Hand finger 5 plays _____.

3. Play each pentascale. Say the finger number as you play each note.

Lesson 8 Review Ultimate Sight Reading & Ear Training Games

1. a) NAME the notes. NAME the pentascale as C Major pentascale or D minor pentascale.

    b) Your Teacher will PLAY each pentascale. Circle the correct Pentascale Pattern (stepping up or stepping down).

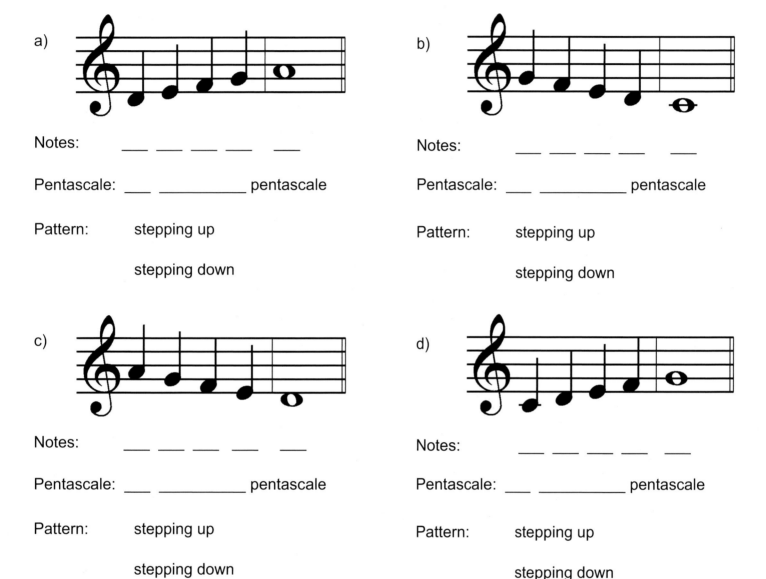

a)

Notes: ___ ___ ___ ___ ___

Pentascale: ___ _____ pentascale

Pattern: stepping up

               stepping down

b)

Notes: ___ ___ ___ ___ ___

Pentascale: ___ _____ pentascale

Pattern: stepping up

               stepping down

c)

Notes: ___ ___ ___ ___ ___

Pentascale: ___ _____ pentascale

Pattern: stepping up

               stepping down

d)

Notes: ___ ___ ___ ___ ___

Pentascale: ___ _____ pentascale

Pattern: stepping up

               stepping down

Imagine, **C**ompose, **E**xplore!

Imagine So-La and Ti-Do are going for a drive on a nice, sunny day.

Compose a song using your Right Hand on the notes of the C Major pentascale.

Explore the happy sounds of the C Major pentascale as they drive up and down the hills.

Imagine that it starts to rain and thunder while So-La and Ti-Do are driving home.

Compose a song using your Right Hand on the notes of the D minor pentascale.

Explore the sad sounds of the D minor pentascale as they drive carefully home through the storm.

BASS CLEF PATTERNS - SAME LINE, SAME SPACE, STEP UP, SKIP UP

So-La Says: Notes in the Bass Clef may be written as Patterns.

Notes:	C	C	C	D	C	E	D	D	D	E	D	F
Pattern:	Same Space		Step Up		Skip Up		Same Line		Step Up		Skip Up	

1. Name the notes. Name the Pattern as: same line, same space, step up or skip up.

Notes: E   F   __   __   __   __   __   __   __   __   __   __

Pattern: step   __   __   __   __   __

              up   __   __   __   __   __

2. Name the notes in the Bass Clef.

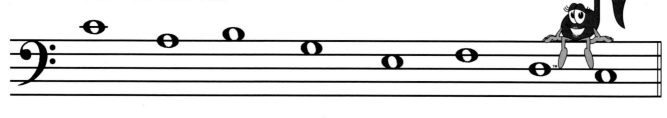

__   __   __   __   __   __   __   __

3. Draw a Bass Clef on the staff. Write the following notes. Use whole notes.
   Use a ruler to draw a ledger line above the Bass Staff when writing the line note Middle C.

Middle C   B   F   A   Bass C   D   G

BASS CLEF PATTERNS - SAME LINE, SAME SPACE, STEP DOWN, SKIP DOWN

So-La Says: Notes in the Bass Clef may be written as Patterns that begin on a line note or a space note.

Notes:	E	E	E	D	E	C	F	F	F	E	F	D
Pattern:	Same Space		Step Down		Skip Down		Same Line		Step Down		Skip Down	

1. Name the notes. Name the Pattern as: same line, same space, step down or skip down.

Notes: E D __ __ __ __ __ __ __ __ __ __

Pattern: step __ __ __ __ __

down __ __ __ __ __

2. Name the notes in the Bass Clef.

__ __ __ __ __ __ __ __ __

3. Draw a Bass Clef on the staff. Write the following notes. Use whole notes.
   Use a ruler to draw a ledger line above the Bass Staff when writing the line note Middle C.

Bass C   F   G   B   E   D   Middle C

BASS CLEF - STEP UP HIGH and SKIP UP HIGH

So-La Says: Music may move in different Patterns of step up high or skip up high. Patterns may be connected by repeating the same note, or by a step (up or down) or by a skip (up or down).

same space
C D E   E G B
step up high   skip up high

step down
D F   A   G A B
skip up high   step up high

1. Patterns: C, D, E is a _____ up high Pattern. E, G, B is a _____ up high Pattern.

   D, F, A is a _____ up high Pattern. G, A, B is a _____ up high Pattern.

2. Following the Pattern, add the missing notes. Use whole notes. Name the missing notes.

Notes: C ___ ___   C ___ ___   E ___ ___   A ___ ___

Pattern: step up high   skip up high   step up high   step up high

3. Name the notes. Draw a line connecting the notes to the keyboard (at the correct pitch).
   Name the Pattern as step up high or skip up high.

Notes: ___ ___ ___   ___ ___ ___   ___ ___ ___

Pattern: _____ up high   _____ up high   _____ up high

BASS CLEF - STEP DOWN LOW and SKIP DOWN LOW

So-La Says: Music may move in different Patterns of step down low or skip down low. Patterns may be connected by repeating the same note, or by a step (up or down) or by a skip (up or down).

skip up

G F E   G E C
step down low   skip down low

step down

C A F   E D C
skip down low   step down low

1. Patterns: G, F, E is a _____ down low Pattern. G, E, C is a _____ down low Pattern.

   C, A, F is a _____ down low Pattern. E, D, C is a _____ down low Pattern.

2. Following the Pattern, add the missing notes. Use whole notes. Name the missing notes.

Notes: C ___ ___   C ___ ___   A ___ ___   E ___ ___

Pattern: step down low   skip down low   skip down low   step down low

3. Name the notes. Draw a line connecting the notes to the keyboard (at the correct pitch).
   Name the Pattern as step down low or skip down low.

Notes: ____ ____ ____   ____ ____ ____   ____ ____ ____

Pattern: _____ down low   _____ down low   _____ down low

BASS CLEF - C MAJOR PENTASCALE PATTERN - MAJOR (HAPPY) SOUND

So-La Says: A Pentascale (penta means 5) is a 5 note scale pattern moving by step.
A PENTASCALE 5 note pattern moves by step in the same direction (up or down).

C pentascale - C, D, E, F, G or G, F, E, D, C - has a HAPPY sound called a MAJOR sound.
C Major pentascale may be written using Whole Notes o and Quarter Notes ♩.

Notes:	C		D	E	F	G	G	F	E	D	C
Pattern:	C		step	up	high	G	G	step	down	low	C

1. A Pentascale (penta means _____) is a _____ note scale pattern moving by _____.

2. C Major pentascale has a happy sound called a _____ sound.

3. Name the notes. Following the pentascale pattern, add the missing notes. Use quarter notes.
   Write the missing note names. Play the C Major pentascale patterns on the piano.

Notes:	___		___	___	___	___	___	___	___	___
Pattern:	C		D	step	up	high	G	step	down	low	C

4. Draw a line connecting the notes to the keyboard (at the correct pitch). Name the C Major
   pentascale pattern as stepping up or stepping down.

C Major pentascale - stepping _____

C Major pentascale - stepping _____

BASS CLEF - D MINOR PENTASCALE PATTERN - MINOR (SAD) SOUND

So-La Says: Pentascale patterns move by step: up (ascending) or down (descending).
A PENTASCALE may have a MAJOR (happy) sound or a MINOR (sad) sound.

D pentascale - D, E, F, G, A or A, G, F, E, D - has a SAD sound called a MINOR sound.

D minor pentascale may be written using Whole Notes o and Quarter Notes ♩.

Notes:	D		E	F	G	A	A	G	F	E		D
Pattern:	D		step	up	high	A	A	step	down	low		D

1. A pentascale may have a _____ (happy) sound or a _____ (sad) sound.

2. D minor pentascale has a sad sound called a _____ sound.

3. Name the notes. Following the pentascale pattern, add the missing notes. Use quarter notes. Write the missing note names. Play the D minor pentascale patterns on the piano.

Notes: ___   ___ ___ ___   ___ ___ ___ ___   ___

Pattern:	D	step	up	high	A	A	step	down	low	D

4. Draw a line connecting the notes to the keyboard (at the correct pitch). Name the D minor pentascale pattern as stepping up or stepping down.

D minor pentascale - stepping _____

D minor pentascale - stepping _____

Lesson 9 Review with So-La & Ti-Do

Check:

1. Fill in the blank to complete each sentence.

   a) A 5 note pattern moving by step in the same direction is called a _____.

   b) C Major pentascale has a happy sound called a _____ sound.

   c) D minor pentascale has a sad sound called a _____ sound.

2. When written in the Bass Clef, the C Major pentascale and the D minor pentascale are usually played with the Left Hand.

   a) Draw a line connecting the notes to the keyboard (at the correct pitch). Name the keys directly on the keyboard.

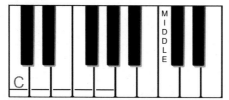

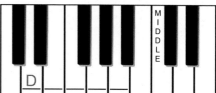

   b) Write the note name for each Finger Number.

When playing the C Major pentascale:

The Left Hand finger 5 plays ___C___.
The Left Hand finger 4 plays _____.
The Left Hand finger 3 plays _____.
The Left Hand finger 2 plays _____.
The Left Hand finger 1 plays _____.

When playing the D minor pentascale:

The Left Hand finger 5 plays ___D___.
The Left Hand finger 4 plays _____.
The Left Hand finger 3 plays _____.
The Left Hand finger 2 plays _____.
The Left Hand finger 1 plays _____.

3. Play each pentascale. Say the finger number as you play each note.

Lesson 9 Review Ultimate Sight Reading & Ear Training Games

Imagine, **C**ompose, **E**xplore!

Imagine So-La and Ti-Do are marching in a Pentascale Parade!

Compose a song about your Pentascale Parade as So-La and Ti-Do march up and down the street with their friends Spot the Dog, Diva the Cat and Max the Turtle.

Explore the different sounds created by the Major pentascale song and the minor pentascale song.

1. COMPOSE a song by adding the missing notes. Follow the pentascale pattern. Use quarter notes. Name the notes.

    PLAY your melody on the piano. Listen to the sound. Write the correct word in the Title.

Title: The _____ Day Pentascale Parade

                                      Sunny or Cloudy

Notes: __   __   __   __   __   __   __   __   __   __

Pattern: G   step - ping   down   low.   C   step - ping   up   high.

Title: The _____ Day Pentascale Parade

                                      Sunny or Cloudy

Notes: __   __   __   __   __   __   __   __   __   __

Pattern: A   step - ping   down   low.   D   step - ping   up   high.

So-La   Ti-Do   Spot   Diva   Max

Lesson 10   Notes Values - Whole, Half & Quarter Notes

TYPES OF NOTES - WHOLE NOTE, HALF NOTE and QUARTER NOTE

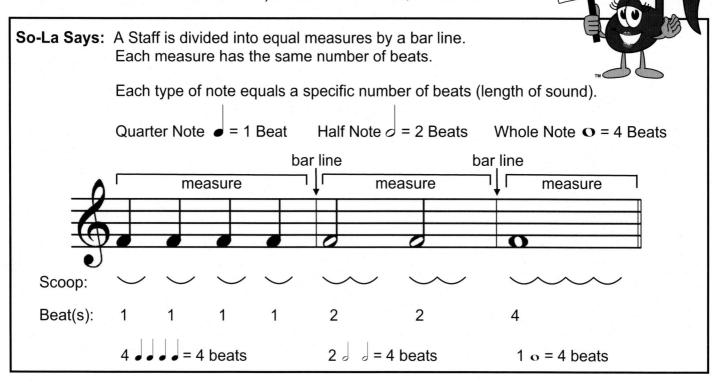

So-La Says: A Staff is divided into equal measures by a bar line.
Each measure has the same number of beats.

Each type of note equals a specific number of beats (length of sound).

Quarter Note ♩ = 1 Beat   Half Note ♩ = 2 Beats   Whole Note 𝅝 = 4 Beats

Scoop:

Beat(s): 1   1   1   1   2   2   4

4 ♩♩♩♩ = 4 beats   2 ♩ ♩ = 4 beats   1 𝅝 = 4 beats

♫ **Ti-Do Tip:** One scoop ‿ is a symbol for one beat of sound. 1 scoop = 1 beat

1. Draw the correct number of scoops below each type of note. Name the notes. Write the number of beats for each note value. Play each melody on the piano.

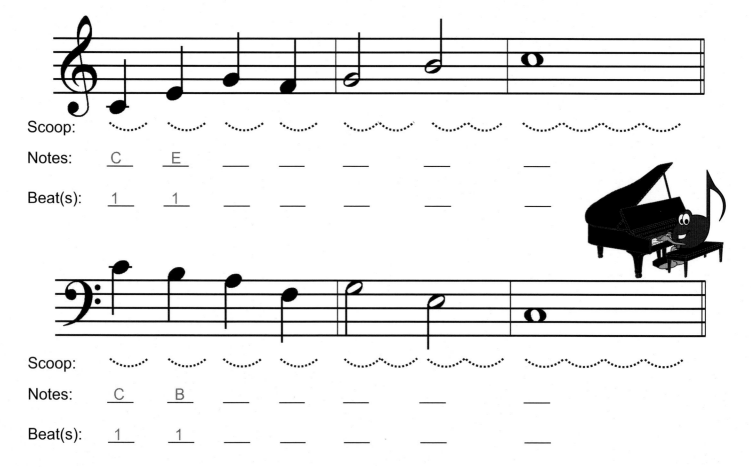

Scoop:

Notes: C   E   ___   ___   ___   ___   ___

Beat(s): 1   1   ___   ___   ___   ___   ___

Scoop:

Notes: C   B   ___   ___   ___   ___   ___

Beat(s): 1   1   ___   ___   ___   ___   ___

NOTE VALUES - WHOLE NOTE, HALF NOTE and QUARTER NOTE

Different TYPES of notes have different NOTE VALUES - specific number of beats of sound.

Quarter Note ♩ also called a "ta" = 1 beat of sound, 1 scoop   ♩ ♩ ♩ ♩ = 4 Beats
                                                                      ta ta ta ta

Half Note ♩ = 2 beats of sound, 2 scoops connected   ♩   ♩ = 4 Beats
                                                         half note half note

Whole Note 𝅝 = 4 beats of sound, 4 scoops connected   𝅝 = 4 Beats
                                                        great big whole note

♫ **Ti-Do Tip:** The number of scoops connected is the number of beats of sound. 2 scoops = 2 beats

1. Fill in the blanks for each type of note and the number of beats of sound for each note.

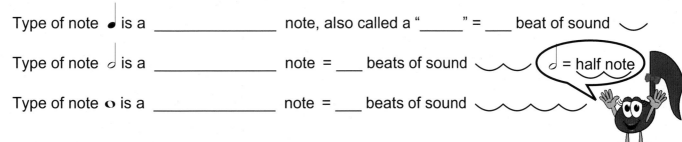

Type of note ♩ is a _____ note, also called a "_____" = ___ beat of sound ⌣

Type of note ♩ is a _____ note = ___ beats of sound ⌣⌣ (♩ = half note)

Type of note 𝅝 is a _____ note = ___ beats of sound ⌣⌣⌣

2. Add scoops (one for each beat) below the following notes.

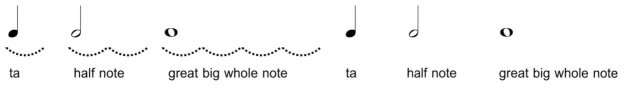

ta   half note   great big whole note   ta   half note   great big whole note

3. Name the type of note as: quarter, half or whole note. Write the number of beats for each note.

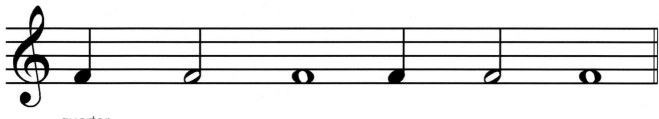

Type: ___quarter___ _____ _____ _____ _____ _____

Beat(s): ___1___ _____ _____ _____ _____ _____

(♩ = ta)

Type: ___whole___ _____ _____ _____ _____ _____

Beat(s): ___4___ _____ _____ _____ _____ _____

TREBLE CLEF - WRITING WHOLE, HALF and QUARTER NOTES

So-La Says: A Whole Note has a circle (oval shape) called a notehead. A Half Note has a line drawn on the side of the notehead called a stem. A Quarter Note has the notehead colored in black.

As seen in music: As drawn by hand:

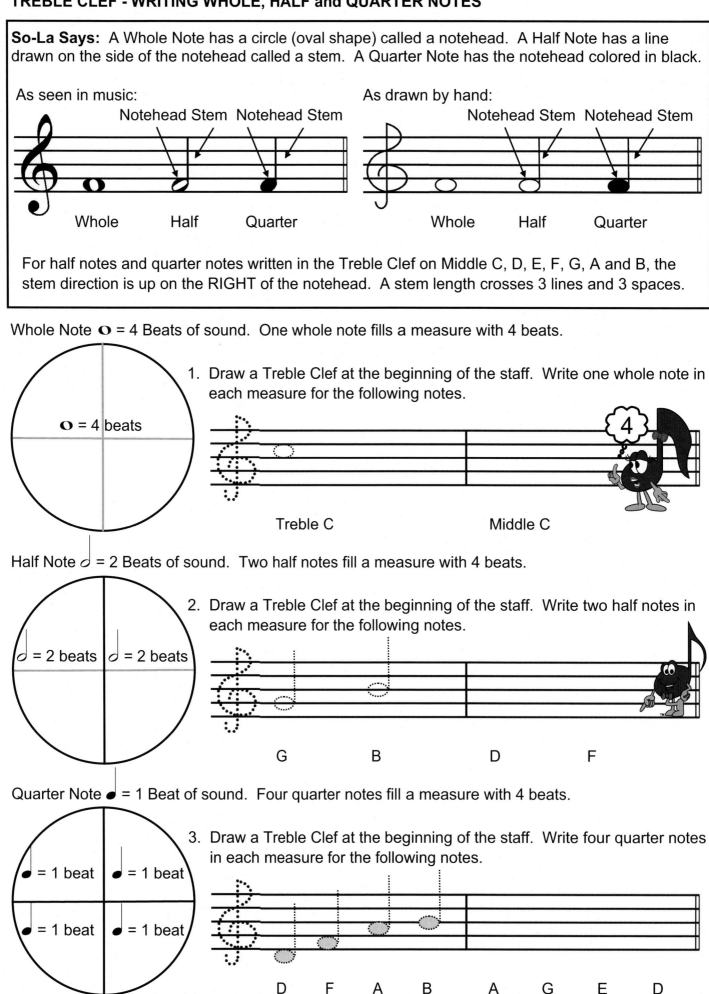

For half notes and quarter notes written in the Treble Clef on Middle C, D, E, F, G, A and B, the stem direction is up on the RIGHT of the notehead. A stem length crosses 3 lines and 3 spaces.

Whole Note 𝅝 = 4 Beats of sound. One whole note fills a measure with 4 beats.

1. Draw a Treble Clef at the beginning of the staff. Write one whole note in each measure for the following notes.

Treble C   Middle C

Half Note 𝅗𝅥 = 2 Beats of sound. Two half notes fill a measure with 4 beats.

2. Draw a Treble Clef at the beginning of the staff. Write two half notes in each measure for the following notes.

G   B   D   F

Quarter Note ♩ = 1 Beat of sound. Four quarter notes fill a measure with 4 beats.

3. Draw a Treble Clef at the beginning of the staff. Write four quarter notes in each measure for the following notes.

D   F   A   B   A   G   E   D

BASS CLEF - WRITING WHOLE, HALF and QUARTER NOTES

So-La Says: A Whole Note has a circle (oval shape) called a notehead. A Half Note has a line drawn on the side of the notehead called a stem. A Quarter Note has the notehead colored in black.

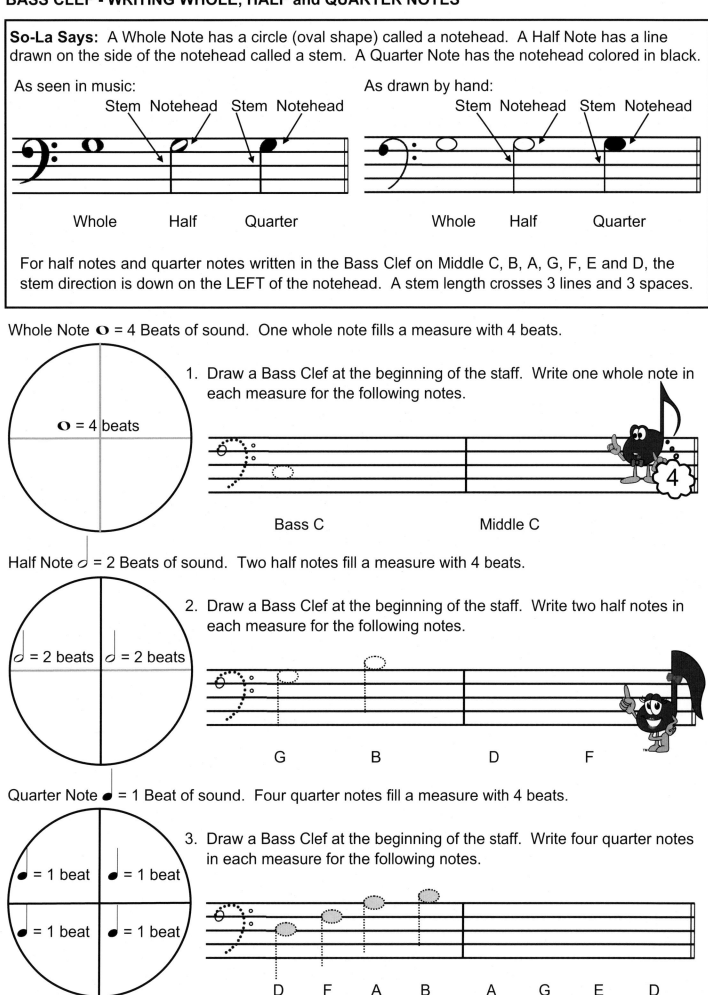

As seen in music:

Stem Notehead   Stem Notehead

Whole   Half   Quarter

As drawn by hand:

Stem Notehead   Stem Notehead

Whole   Half   Quarter

For half notes and quarter notes written in the Bass Clef on Middle C, B, A, G, F, E and D, the stem direction is down on the LEFT of the notehead. A stem length crosses 3 lines and 3 spaces.

Whole Note 𝐨 = 4 Beats of sound. One whole note fills a measure with 4 beats.

𝐨 = 4 beats

1. Draw a Bass Clef at the beginning of the staff. Write one whole note in each measure for the following notes.

Bass C   Middle C

Half Note ♩ = 2 Beats of sound. Two half notes fill a measure with 4 beats.

♩ = 2 beats ♩ = 2 beats

2. Draw a Bass Clef at the beginning of the staff. Write two half notes in each measure for the following notes.

G   B   D   F

Quarter Note ♩ = 1 Beat of sound. Four quarter notes fill a measure with 4 beats.

♩ = 1 beat ♩ = 1 beat

♩ = 1 beat ♩ = 1 beat

3. Draw a Bass Clef at the beginning of the staff. Write four quarter notes in each measure for the following notes.

D F A B   A G E D

C MAJOR PENTASCALE - MELODY and RHYTHM

A MELODY has a RHYTHM (different note values) divided into equal measures of beats.

Melody: Notes moving by patterns (same, step, skip) based on notes from pentascales.
Rhythm: Note values (whole, half and quarter notes) with equal beats in each measure.

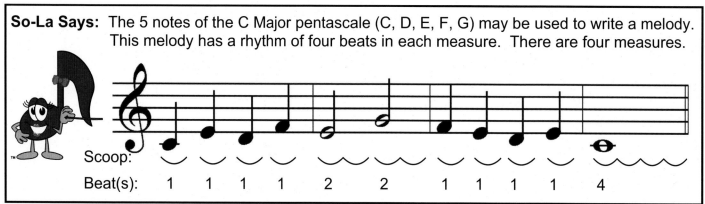

So-La Says: The 5 notes of the C Major pentascale (C, D, E, F, G) may be used to write a melody. This melody has a rhythm of four beats in each measure. There are four measures.

Scoop:

Beat(s):   1   1   1   1   2   2   1   1   1   1   4

1. Fill in the blanks:

Melody is notes moving by _____ (same, step, skip) based on notes from pentascales.

Rhythm is note _____ (whole, half and quarter notes) with equal beats in each measure.

The 5 notes of the C Major pentascale (___, ___, ___, ___, ___) may be used to write a melody.

2. Draw the scoop(s) below each note. Name the notes. Write the number of beats for each note.
    Play each melody. Listen for the happy sound of the melodies based on the C Major pentascale.

Scoop:

Notes: G   ___   ___   ___   ___   ___   ___   ___   ___   ___   ___

Beat(s): 1   ___   ___   ___   ___   ___   ___   ___   ___   ___   ___

Scoop:

Notes: G   ___   ___   ___   ___   ___   ___   ___   ___   ___

Beat(s): 1   ___   ___   ___   ___   ___   ___   ___   ___   ___

D MINOR PENTASCALE - MELODY and RHYTHM

A MELODY has different patterns (same, step, skip) and different RHYTHMS (note values) divided into equal measures of beats. A melody may have a happy sound or a sad sound.

A Major pentascale melody has a happy sound. A minor pentascale melody has a sad sound.

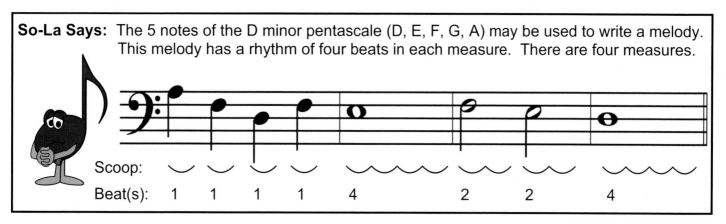

So-La Says: The 5 notes of the D minor pentascale (D, E, F, G, A) may be used to write a melody. This melody has a rhythm of four beats in each measure. There are four measures.

Scoop:
Beat(s):   1   1   1   1   4   2   2   4

1. Fill in the blanks:

A melody has different patterns and different rhythms divided into equal _____ of beats.

A Major pentascale melody has a _____ sound. A minor pentascale melody has a _____ sound.

The 5 notes of the D minor pentascale (___, ___, ___, ___, ___) may be used to write a melody.

2. Draw the scoop(s) below each note. Name the notes. Write the number of beats for each note.
    Play each melody. Listen for the sad sound of the melodies based on the D minor pentascale.

Scoop:

Notes: A   ___   ___   ___   ___   ___   ___   ___   ___

Beat(s): 2   ___   ___   ___   ___   ___   ___   ___   ___

Scoop:

Notes: D   ___   ___   ___   ___   ___   ___   ___

Beat(s): 2   ___   ___   ___   ___   ___   ___   ___

Lesson 10 Review with So-La & Ti-Do

1. Identify each Musical Concept by filling in the blanks. Use the following words (terms):

   Measure   Treble Clef   Bar Line   Notehead   Stem Up

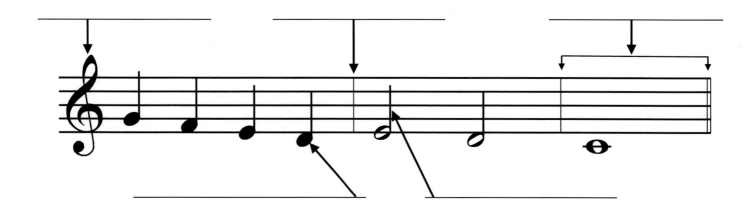

2. Identify each Musical Concept by filling in the blanks. Use the following words (terms):

   Whole Note   Half Note   Quarter Note   Ledger Line   Bass Clef

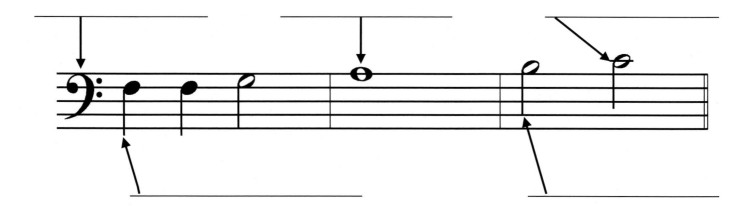

3. Name the notes. Write the number of beats for each note value. Play the melody on the piano.

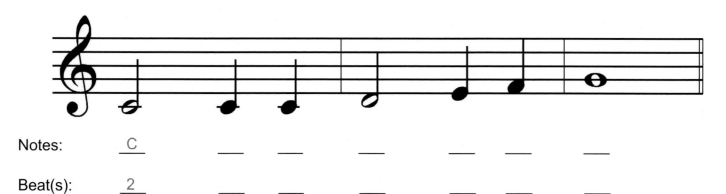

Notes: <u>C</u>   ___   ___   ___   ___   ___   ___

Beat(s):   <u>2</u>   ___   ___   ___   ___   ___   ___

Lesson 10 Review Ultimate Sight Reading & Ear Training Games

1. Have a Pizza Party! WRITE the missing note(s) and beat(s) to complete each Pizza with 4 beats.

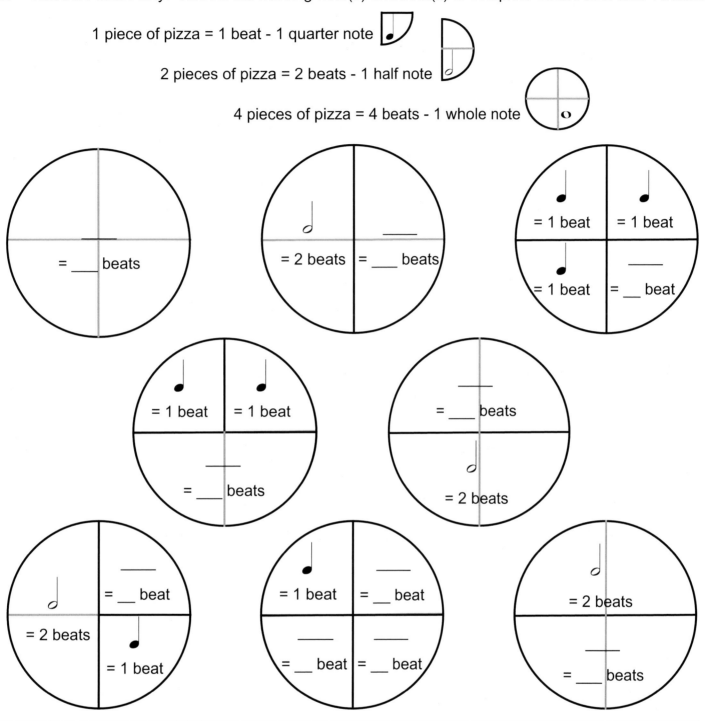

1 piece of pizza = 1 beat - 1 quarter note

2 pieces of pizza = 2 beats - 1 half note

4 pieces of pizza = 4 beats - 1 whole note

= ___ beats

= 2 beats   = ___ beats

= 1 beat   = 1 beat
= 1 beat   = __ beat

= 1 beat   = 1 beat
= ___ beats

= ___ beats
= 2 beats

= ___ beat
= 2 beats
= 1 beat

= 1 beat   = __ beat
= __ beat   = __ beat

= 2 beats
= ___ beats

Imagine, **C**ompose, **E**xplore!

Imagine So-La and Ti-Do are having a
Pizza Party and YOU are invited!

Compose a song using the notes of the C Major pentascale
(C, D, E, F, G) or the D minor pentascale (D, E, F, G, A).

Explore the happy (C Major pentascale) sound if your pizza is hot and fresh.
Explore the sad (D minor pentascale) sound if your pizza is cold and stale.

Lesson 11   Time Signature - Simple Time

TIME SIGNATURE - NUMBER OF EQUAL BEATS PER MEASURE

A Time Signature is written on the staff after the clef. Two numbers are used for a Time Signature, one above the other. The Time Signature $\frac{4}{4}$ is called Simple Time.

So-La Says: In Simple Time, the Time Signature $\frac{4}{4}$ has two numbers.

4 Top number **4** means 4 beats per measure. Each measure has 4 beats.

4 Bottom number **4** means a quarter note equals 1 beat. Each measure is counted 1, 2, 3, 4.

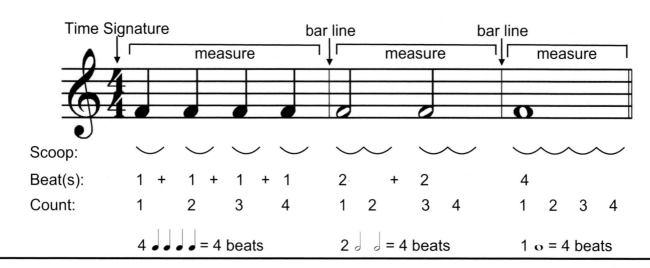

♫ **Ti-Do Tip:** In $\frac{4}{4}$ time, each measure contains 4 beats. A quarter note equals one beat.

1. Write the counts (1, 2, 3, 4) below the notes in each measure.

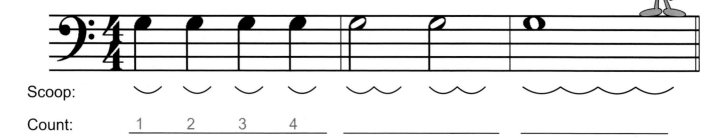

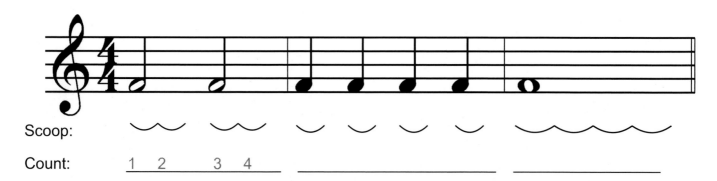

TIME SIGNATURE and RHYTHM

The TIME SIGNATURE $\frac{4}{4}$ indicates 4 beats per measure and a quarter note equals 1 beat.
The RHYTHM in each measure may be different types of notes that equal 4 beats in each measure.

So-La Says: In $\frac{4}{4}$ time, each measure has 4 beats. Different types of notes (quarter notes and/or half notes) may be combined to equal 4 beats. A whole note fills a whole measure with 4 beats.

1 whole note = 4 beats of sound (great big whole note)
Beat(s): 4 — Counts: 1 2 3 4

2 half notes = 4 beats of sound (half note, half note)
Beat(s): 2 + 2 — Counts: 1 2 3 4

4 quarter notes = 4 beats of sound (ta, ta, ta, ta)
Beat(s): 1 + 1 + 1 + 1 — Counts: 1 2 3 4

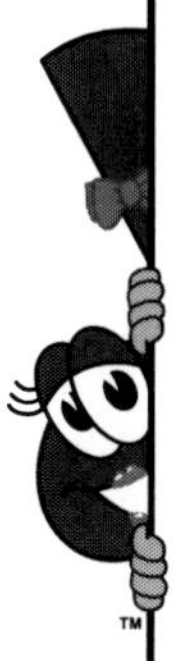

1. Complete the following Note Value Chart.

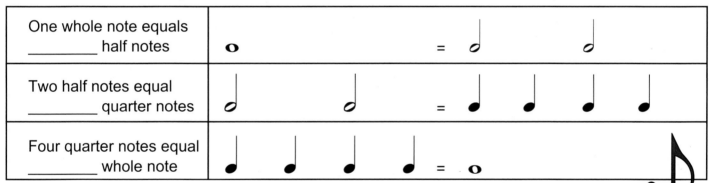

One whole note equals ________ half notes	whole note = half note, half note
Two half notes equal ________ quarter notes	half note, half note = quarter note, quarter note, quarter note, quarter note
Four quarter notes equal ________ whole note	quarter note, quarter note, quarter note, quarter note = whole note

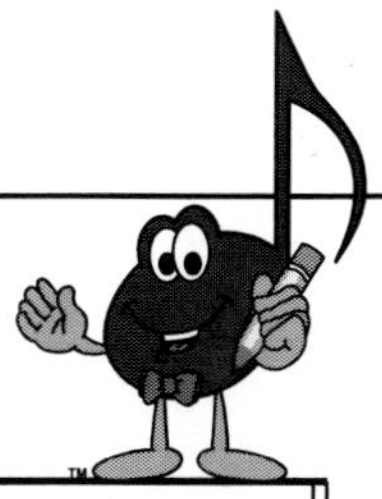

2. Write the counts (1, 2, 3, 4) below the notes in each measure.

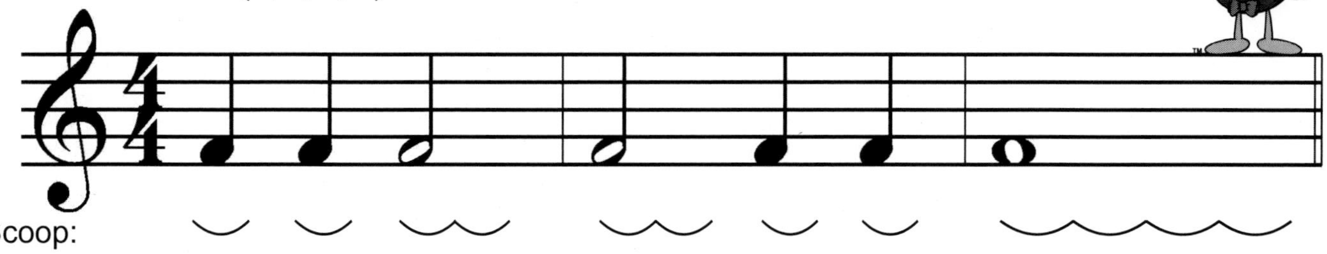

Scoop:

Count: 1 2 3 4 ________ ________

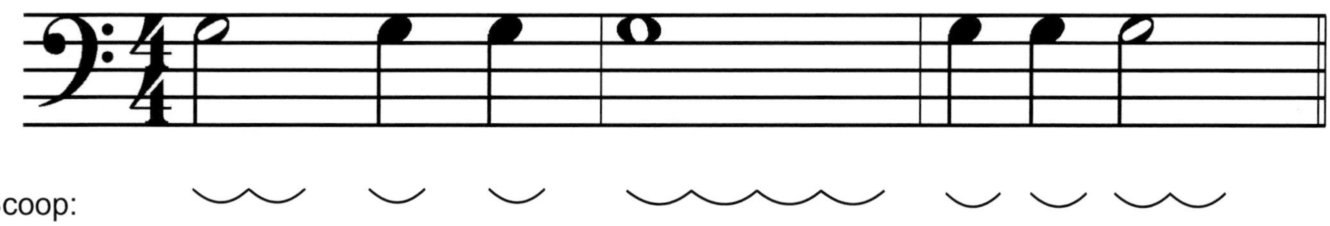

Scoop:

Count: 1 2 3 4 ________ ________

TIME SIGNATURE - ADDING BAR LINES

In $\frac{4}{4}$ time, the rhythm in each measure equals 4 beats. Each measure is divided by a BAR LINE.

So-La Says: A BAR LINE is a straight line from the top of the staff (line 5) to the bottom (line 1). In $\frac{4}{4}$ time, a bar line divides the rhythm in each measure into 4 equal beats.

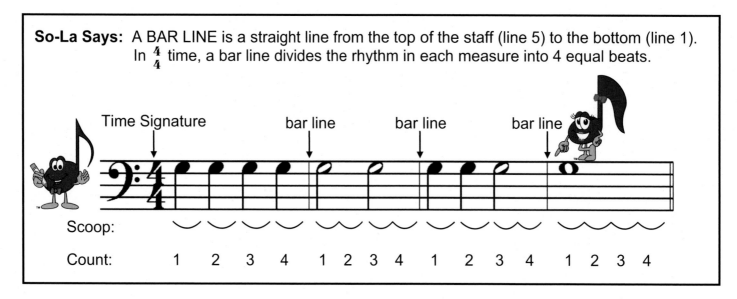

♫ **Ti-Do Tip:** Use a ruler to draw straight bar lines on the staff from the top line 5 down to line 1.

1. The Time Signature is $\frac{4}{4}$. Add bar lines to divide the staff into equal measures of 4 beats.

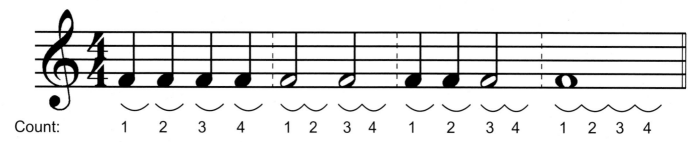

Count: 1   2   3   4   1   2   3 4   1   2   3 4   1   2   3   4

2. Write the counts (1, 2, 3, 4) below the notes. Add bar lines to create equal measures in $\frac{4}{4}$ time.

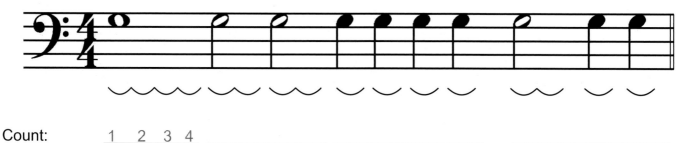

Count: 1   2   3   4 _____ _____   _____

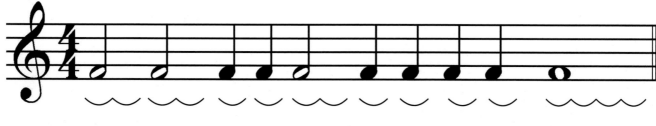

Count: 1   2   3   4 _____ _____   _____

TIME SIGNATURE - ADDING NOTE VALUES

In $\frac{4}{4}$ time, the note values in each measure equal 4 beats. Each type of note has a NOTE VALUE.

So-La Says: A NOTE VALUE is indicated by the type of note. Each type of note has a note value.

In $\frac{4}{4}$ time, each measure has note values adding up to 4 beats. When ONE note is missing for:

1 beat = add a quarter note. 2 beats = add a half note. 4 beats = add a whole note.

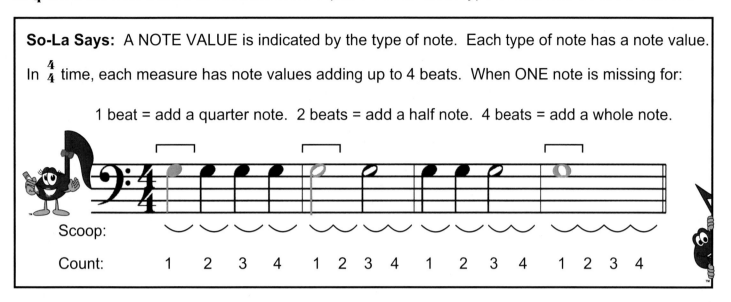

Scoop:

Count: 1   2   3   4   1   2   3   4   1   2   3   4   1   2   3   4

♫ **Ti-Do Tip:** Count the number of beats in each measure to determine the missing note value.

1. The Time Signature is $\frac{4}{4}$. Add one note below each bracket to create equal measures of 4 beats.

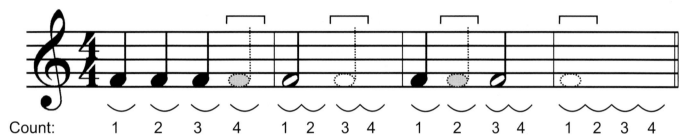

Count: 1   2   3   4   1   2   3   4   1   2   3   4   1   2   3   4

2. Write the counts (1, 2, 3, 4) below the notes. Add one note to create equal measures in $\frac{4}{4}$ time.

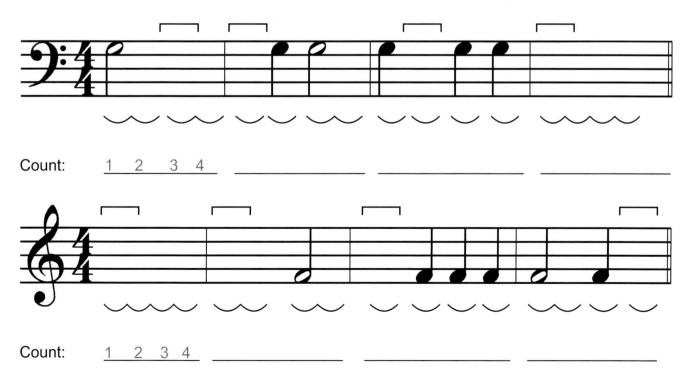

Count: 1   2   3   4   _____   _____   _____

Count: 1   2   3   4   _____   _____   _____

C MAJOR PENTASCALE - MELODY, TIME SIGNATURE and RHYTHM

A melody may be written in the Treble Clef or the Bass Clef. The Time Signature $\frac{4}{4}$ means the rhythm (different note values) is divided into equal measures of 4 beats separated by a bar line.

So-La Says: A melody may be written based on the notes of the C Major pentascale (C, D, E, F, G). A melody written using the 5 notes of the C Major pentascale has a happy sound.

Notes:	E	E	D	F	E	G	F	E	D	E	C
Count:	1	2	3	4	1	2	3	4	1	2	3	4	1 2 3 4

1. Fill in the blanks: A melody using the 5 notes of the C Major pentascale has a _____ sound.

A melody may be written in the _____ Clef or the _____ Clef.

The Time Signature $\frac{4}{4}$ means the rhythm is divided into equal measures of ____ beats.

A melody may be written using the 5 notes of the C Major pentascale: ___, ___, ___, ___, ___.

2. For each melody: Name the notes. Write the counts below each measure. Play each melody. Listen for the happy sound of the melodies based on the notes of the C Major pentascale.

Notes: E __ __ __ __ __ __ __ __ __ __ __

Count: 1 _____ _____ _____

Notes: C __ __ __ __ __ __ __

Count: 1 2 3 4 _____ _____ _____

D MINOR PENTASCALE - MELODY, TIME SIGNATURE and RHYTHM

A melody may be written with different patterns and different rhythms divided into equal measures.
A melody based on: C Major pentascale has a happy sound; D minor pentascale has a sad sound.

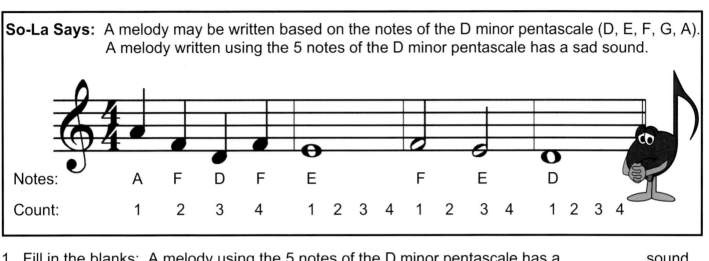

So-La Says: A melody may be written based on the notes of the D minor pentascale (D, E, F, G, A).
A melody written using the 5 notes of the D minor pentascale has a sad sound.

Notes: A F D F E   F E D

Count: 1 2 3 4   1 2 3 4 1 2 3 4   1 2 3 4

1. Fill in the blanks: A melody using the 5 notes of the D minor pentascale has a _____ sound.

A melody may be written with different _____ and different _____ divided into equal measures.

A melody in C _____ pentascale has a happy sound, in D _____ pentascale has a sad sound.

A melody may be written using the 5 notes of the D minor pentascale: ___, ___, ___, ___, ___.

2. For each melody: Name the notes. Write the counts below each measure. Play each melody.
    Listen for the sad sound of the melodies based on the notes of the D minor pentascale.

Notes: D ___ ___   ___ ___ ___   ___ ___ ___ ___ ___

Count: 1 _____ _____ _____ _____

Notes: D ___ ___ ___ ___ ___   ___ ___ ___ ___

Count: 1 2 _____ _____ _____ _____

Lesson 11   Review with So-La & Ti-Do

1.   For each melody: Name the notes. Write the missing note below each bracket. Use the correct note value (quarter, half or whole). Play the melody on the piano. Circle the correct answer to each question below.

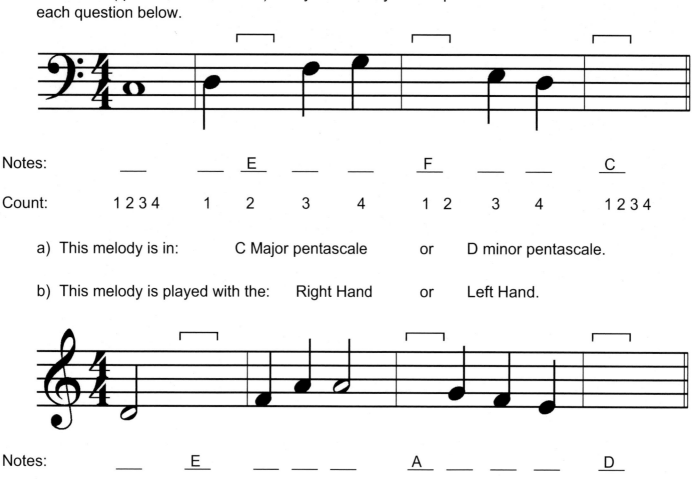

Notes: ___   ___   E   ___   ___   F   ___   ___   C

Count: 1 2 3 4   1   2   3   4   1 2   3   4   1 2 3 4

a) This melody is in: C Major pentascale   or   D minor pentascale.

b) This melody is played with the: Right Hand   or   Left Hand.

Notes: ___   E   ___   ___   ___   A   ___   ___   ___   D

Count: 1 2   3 4   1   2   3 4   1   2   3   4   1 2 3 4

c) This melody is in: C Major pentascale   or   D minor pentascale.

d) This melody is played with the: Right Hand   or   Left Hand.

2.   Draw the scoop(s) below each note. Write the counts (1, 2, 3, 4) below the notes. Add bar lines to create equal measures.

Scoop:

Count: _____   _____   _____   _____

Lesson 11 Review Ultimate Sight Reading & Ear Training Games

1.   a) NAME the notes. WRITE the counts below the notes.

       b) Your Teacher will play one melody from each question. Listen to the rhythm.
           CIRCLE the correct melody.

a)

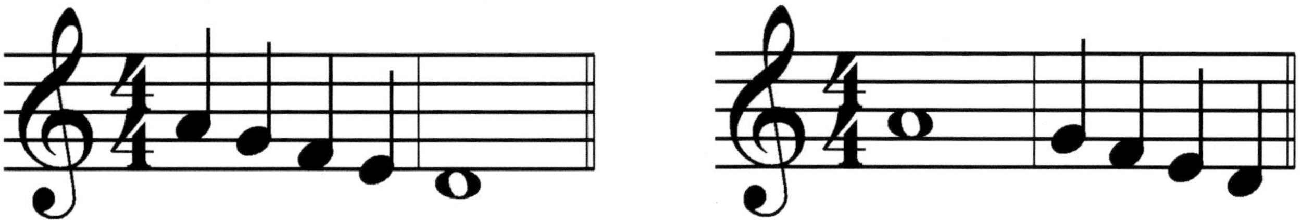

Notes: __ __ __ __ __   __ __ __ __ __

Count: _____ _____   _____ _____

b)

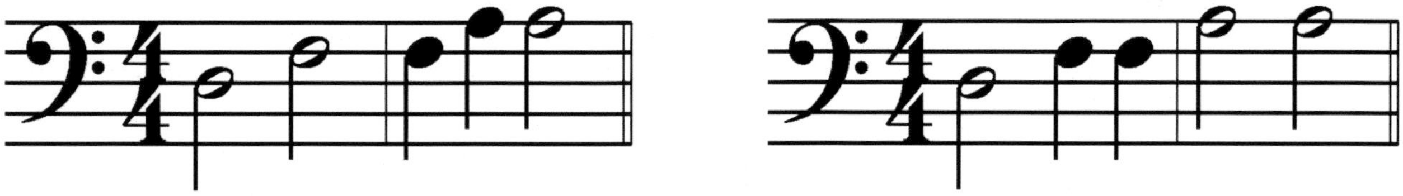

Notes: __ __ __ __ __   __ __ __ __ __

Count: _____ _____   _____ _____

c)

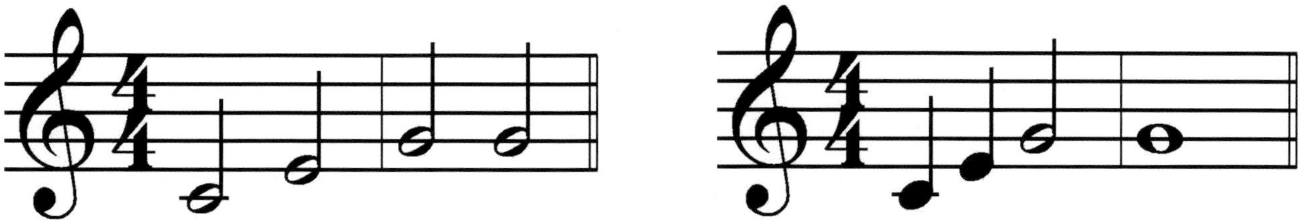

Notes: __ __ __ __   __ __ __ __

Count: _____ _____   _____ _____

d)

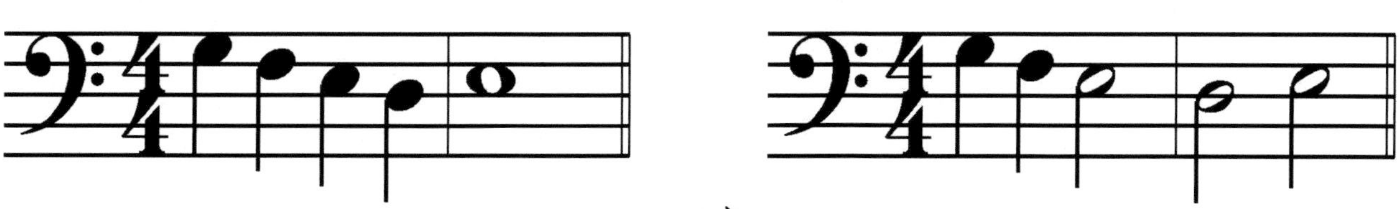

Notes: __ __ __ __ __   __ __ __ __ __

Count: _____ _____   _____ _____

Lesson 12   Italian Terms - Dynamics & Articulation

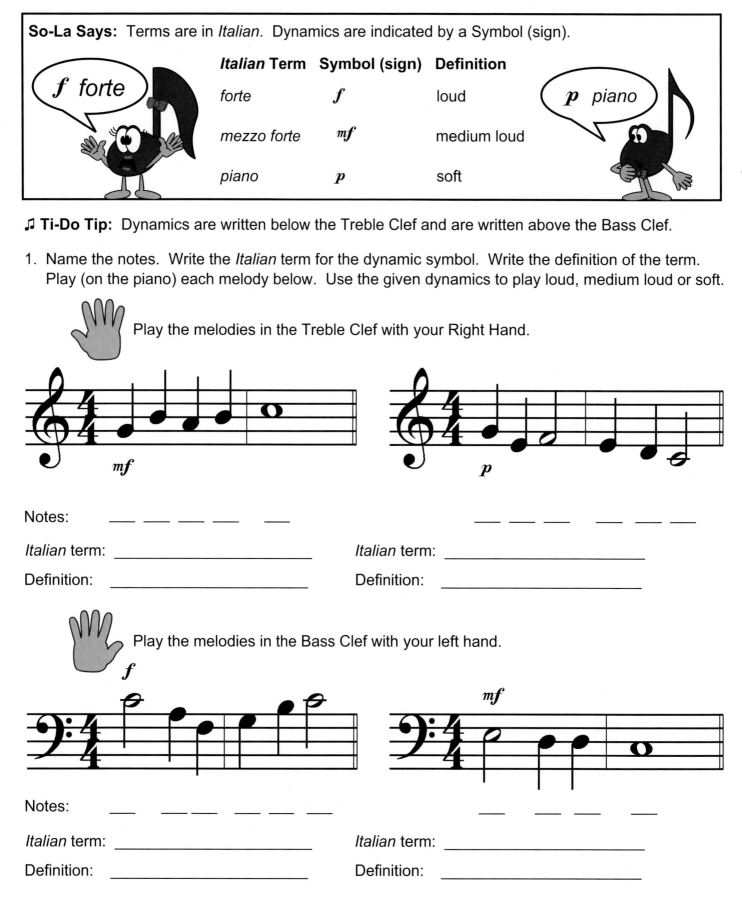

DYNAMICS - FORTE (LOUD), MEZZO FORTE (MEDIUM LOUD), PIANO (SOFT)

Italian terms, symbols or signs are used to indicate how music is to be played.
DYNAMICS are signs that indicate the VOLUME (loud, medium loud, soft) of sound.

So-La Says: Terms are in *Italian*. Dynamics are indicated by a Symbol (sign).

f forte

p piano

Italian Term	Symbol (sign)	Definition
forte	*f*	loud
mezzo forte	*mf*	medium loud
piano	*p*	soft

♫ **Ti-Do Tip:** Dynamics are written below the Treble Clef and are written above the Bass Clef.

1. Name the notes. Write the *Italian* term for the dynamic symbol. Write the definition of the term.
   Play (on the piano) each melody below. Use the given dynamics to play loud, medium loud or soft.

Play the melodies in the Treble Clef with your Right Hand.

mf

p

Notes: __ __ __ __ __   __ __ __ __ __ __

Italian term: _____   *Italian* term: _____

Definition: _____   Definition: _____

Play the melodies in the Bass Clef with your left hand.

f

mf

Notes: __ __ __ __ __   __ __ __ __

Italian term: _____   *Italian* term: _____

Definition: _____   Definition: _____

ARTICULATION - LEGATO, SLUR (SMOOTH) and STACCATO (SHARPLY DETACHED)

Italian Terms, symbols or signs are used in music to show expression in the melody.
ARTICULATION are signs that indicate the TOUCH (smooth or detached), how the notes are played.

So-La Says: *Italian* terms for Articulation are indicated by a Symbol (sign).

	Italian Term	Symbol (sign)	Definition
The Italian term *legato* means smooth. A smooth curved line called a slur is a sign to play the notes *legato* (smooth).	*legato* (slur)		smooth (play notes *legato)*
The Italian term *staccato* means detached. A dot above or below the notehead means to play the note sharply detached (not smooth).	*staccato* (dot)		detached (sharply detached)

♫ **Ti-Do Tip:** Articulation is written close to the notehead and away from the stems.

1. Name the notes. Write the *Italian* term for the articulation symbol. Write the definition of the term. Play (on the piano) each melody below. Use the given articulation to play smooth or detached.

Play the melodies in the Treble Clef with your Right Hand.

Notes: __ __ __ __ __ __   __ __ __ __ __ __

Italian term: _____   *Italian* term: _____

Definition: _____   Definition: _____

Play the melodies in the Bass Clef with your Left Hand.

Notes: __ __ __ __ __   __ __ __ __ __ __

Italian term: _____   *Italian* term: _____

Definition: _____   Definition: _____

MELODY - MAJOR and MINOR - DYNAMICS and ARTICULATION

Music has a melody (Major - happy sound or minor - sad sound), patterns (same, skip, step),
rhythm (note values), dynamics (volume) and articulation (touch) that express a feeling, idea or story.

So-La Says: *Italian* terms, symbols or signs add expression with dynamics and articulation.

Italian Term	Symbol (sign)	Definition	Italian Term	Symbol (sign)	Definition
forte	*f*	loud	legato (slur)		smooth / play notes *legato*
mezzo forte	*mf*	medium loud			
piano	*p*	soft	staccato (dot)		sharply detached / play notes detached

♫ **Ti-Do Tip:** Learn. Play. Listen. Learn the Italian terms. Play each melody below. Listen for the sound of Major or minor, patterns and direction, rhythm, dynamics and articulation.

1. Answer the questions below each melody.

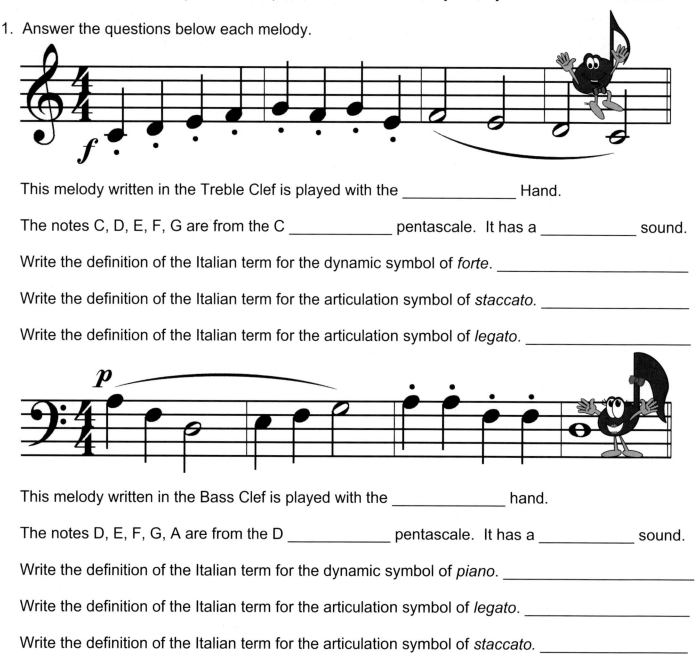

This melody written in the Treble Clef is played with the _____ Hand.

The notes C, D, E, F, G are from the C _____ pentascale. It has a _____ sound.

Write the definition of the Italian term for the dynamic symbol of *forte*. _____

Write the definition of the Italian term for the articulation symbol of *staccato*. _____

Write the definition of the Italian term for the articulation symbol of *legato*. _____

This melody written in the Bass Clef is played with the _____ hand.

The notes D, E, F, G, A are from the D _____ pentascale. It has a _____ sound.

Write the definition of the Italian term for the dynamic symbol of *piano*. _____

Write the definition of the Italian term for the articulation symbol of *legato*. _____

Write the definition of the Italian term for the articulation symbol of *staccato*. _____

ANALYSIS and PLAYING MUSIC

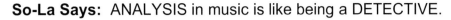

 So-La Says: ANALYSIS in music is like being a DETECTIVE.

Analysis is looking for clues in music. Analysis helps us learn how to read music faster and play music easier.

Be a detective. Look for the TOP 10 Clues!

♫ **Ti-Do Tip:** Read the question carefully. Use the Detective Clues to find the correct answer.

#1 Landmark: Treble Clef - Middle C, G, C. Bass Clef - Middle C, F, C

#2 Direction: Patterns - same note, step or skip (up or down)

#3 Note Values: Whole = 4 beats, Half = 2 beats, Quarter = 1 beat

1. Bass Clef landmark notes are Middle ____, Bass ____ and Bass ____.

2. In $\frac{4}{4}$ time: Half Note = ____ beats and a Whole Note = ____ beats.

3. The direction of a pattern moving by step or skip may be _____ or _____.

#4 Pentascales: C Major (C, D, E, F, G) or D minor (D, E, F, G, A)

#5 Patterns: 3 or more notes may be stepping up or stepping down

#6 Rhythm: Different note values may be used for each equal measure

4. Each measure has _____ beats. One Quarter Note = ____ beat.

5. The pattern moving down from G to C is called a _____ down pattern.

6. The notes G, F, E, D, C are the notes of the C _____ pentascale.

#7 Clef: Treble Clef (RH) and Bass Clef (LH)

#8 Time Signature number: Top - 4 beats per measure, Bottom - ♩ = 1 beat

#9 Articulation: *legato* (smooth), *staccato* (sharply detached)

#10 Dynamics: *forte* (loud), *mezzo forte* (medium loud), *piano* (soft)

7. Notes in the Bass Clef are played with the _____ Hand.

8. Time Signature $\frac{4}{4}$, the top number 4 means _____ beats in a measure.

9. Italian term for the dot above a note to play sharply detached is _____.

10. Definition of the dynamic term *mezzo forte* means to play _____.

Lesson 12   Review with So-La & Ti-Do

Check:

1. Write the notes of the C Major pentascale in the Bass Clef and in the Treble Clef. Use whole notes. Draw a line from each note in the Bass Staff and Treble Staff to the key on the keyboard (at the correct pitch). Name the key directly on the keyboard.

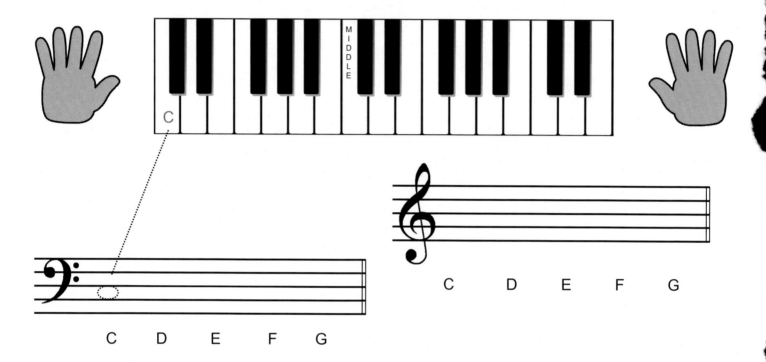

2. Write the notes of the D minor pentascale in the Bass Clef and in the Treble Clef. Use whole notes. Draw a line from each note in the Bass Staff and Treble Staff to the key on the keyboard (at the correct pitch). Name the key directly on the keyboard.

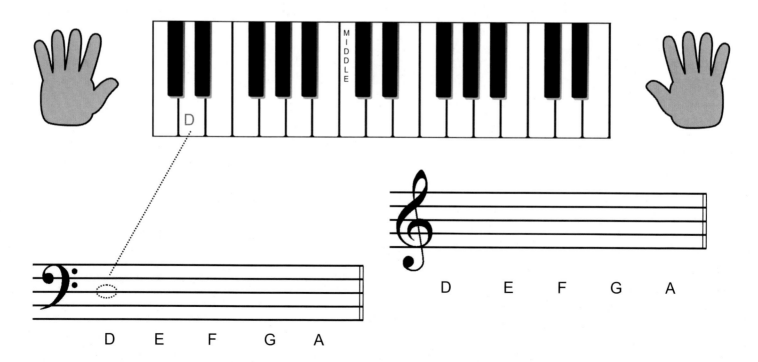

Lesson 12 Review Ultimate Sight Reading & Ear Training Games

1.   LISTEN as your Teacher plays each song on the piano. Name the pattern direction as: step up, step down, skip up, skip down or same sound. Name the dynamics as *forte*, *mezzo forte* or *piano*. Name the articulation as *legato* or *staccato*.

2.   With your Teacher, PLAY (on the piano) and SING each song.

The C Major Pentascale Song

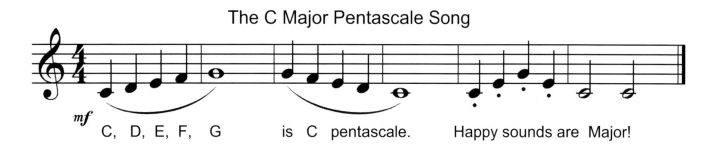

mf   C, D, E, F,   G   is C pentascale.   Happy sounds are Major!

The D minor Pentascale Song

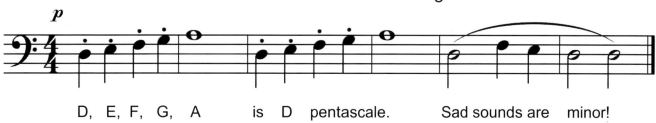

D, E, F, G, A   is D pentascale.   Sad sounds are   minor!

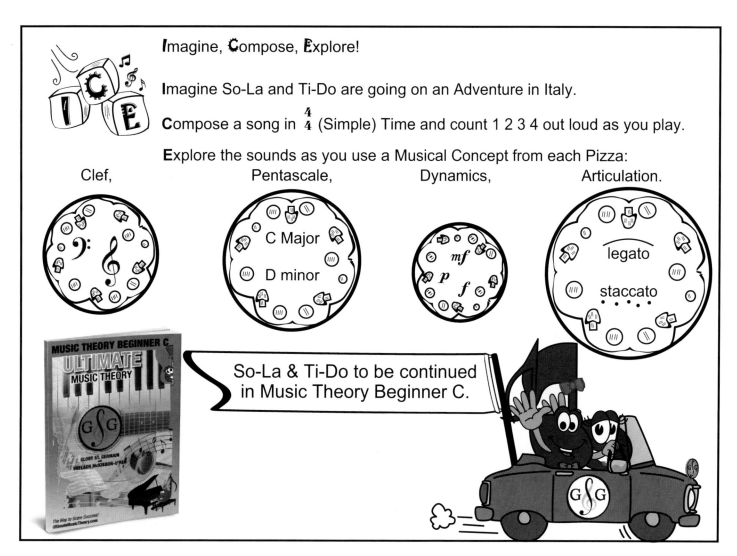

Imagine, **C**ompose, **E**xplore!

Imagine So-La and Ti-Do are going on an Adventure in Italy.

Compose a song in $\frac{4}{4}$ (Simple) Time and count 1 2 3 4 out loud as you play.

Explore the sounds as you use a Musical Concept from each Pizza:

Clef,   Pentascale,   Dynamics,   Articulation.

So-La & Ti-Do to be continued in Music Theory Beginner C.

Ultimate Music Theory Certificate

_____

has successfully completed all the requirements of the

Music Theory Beginner B

_____

Music Teacher

Date

Enriching Lives Through Music Education